UNIVERSITY OF

turn this book as

ON TOP OF
THE WORLD

Recent Titles in
Contributions in Women's Studies

ON TOP OF THE WORLD

Women's Political Leadership in Scandinavia and Beyond

Bruce O. Solheim

Contributions in Women's Studies, Number 177

GREENWOOD PRESS
Westport, Connecticut • London

Library of Congress Cataloging-in-Publication Data

Solheim, Bruce Olav.
    On top of the world : women's political leadership in Scandinavia
and beyond / Bruce O. Solheim.
       p.   cm.—(Contributions in women's studies, ISSN 0147–104X ;
no. 177)
    Includes bibliographical references and index.
    ISBN 0–313–31000–9 (alk. paper)
    1. Women in politics—Scandinavia. 2. Women politicians—
Scandinavia. 3. Leadership in women. 4. Political leadership—Sex
differences. I. Title. II. Series.
HQ1236.5.S34S65 2000
320'.082'0948—dc21   99–15393

British Library Cataloguing in Publication Data is available.

Library of Congress Catalog Card Number: 99–15393
ISBN: 0–313–31000–9
ISSN: 0147–104X

First published in 2000

Greenwood Press, 88 Post Road West, Westport, CT 06881
An imprint of Greenwood Publishing Group, Inc.
www.greenwood.com

Printed in the United States of America

The paper used in this book complies with the
Permanent Paper Standard issued by the National
Information Standards Organization (Z39.48–1984).

10 9 8 7 6 5 4 3 2 1

Contents

Tables and Figures

TABLES

FIGURES

Preface

The Glory of Creation is in its infinite diversity and in the ways our differences combine to create meaning and beauty.
　　—Spock, from the Star Trek episode, "Is There in Truth, No Beauty?"

My interest in the topic of women in power was generated, in part, by my experiences in the military. As a military officer I was expected to exhibit certain leadership qualities. The problem was that my less strident style of leadership, using cooperation and persuasion rather than intimidation, did not please my superior officers. I was criticized for my apparent lack of aggressiveness. Eventually, I left the military only to end up in the paramilitary world of corporate America. As an administrator with a major corporation, I was one of several young men being groomed for future management. One day my boss took me aside and said: "Your work is excellent, but you need to be more aggressive." He went on to compare me to another young administrator. "He is no better in terms of knowledge, skill, or results, but he is more aggressive than you," my boss said. Apparently, both the military and large corporations found aggressiveness a necessary attribute for leadership. Only later did I come to realize that I was fighting the androcentric power structure that has dominated our society. My natural tendency toward a more cooperative, nonaggressive style of leadership—despite my gender—was found to be unacceptable.

To reinforce the lesson, I discovered after my mother passed away in 1990 that her leadership in the family was clearly missed. We were not the same without her. Her style of behind-the-scenes leadership and subtle use of power was not apparent to me before. The more I thought about it, the more it made sense. She had learned to wield power in a way that allowed my father to appear to be on top and in charge. This intriguing discovery is key to my interest in alternative forms of leadership and to the role of women in politics.

I wish to acknowledge all those people who lent their support, guidance, and effort toward the successful completion of this book. The Norwegian Foreign Ministry provided a travel grant that enabled me to conduct research in Norway. I am also indebted to Norwegian Parliament member Erna Solberg who gave me insights into the political system in Norway and shared her personal experiences as a woman politician. I also learned a great deal from an International Women's Leadership Conference that Green River Community College sponsored in 1995. I also wish to extend my gratitude to Pat Zenone, a reference librarian at Citrus College who assisted me in obtaining materials for my final research. My wife Heather has read the manuscript many times and I am eternally grateful for her love, advice, and suggestions. Finally, I wish to thank the editorial staff at Greenwood Publishing Group for their professionalism and kind attention.

Chapter 1

Equality or Difference?: Women Leaders in World Politics

> To call woman the weaker sex is a libel; it is man's injustice to woman. If by strength is meant brute strength, then indeed is woman less brute than man. If by strength is meant moral power, then woman is immeasurably man's superior. Has she not greater intuition, is she not more self-sacrificing, has she not greater power of endurance, has she not greater courage? Without her man could not be. If non-violence is the law of our being, the future is with woman.
> —Mohandas K. Gandhi

OVERVIEW

Since 1989 many people have celebrated the defeat of communism and the triumph of democracy. Freedom rings out in the hearts of people formerly subjected to tyranny. Essential to this freedom and fundamental to democracy is the right of voting and equitable representation in government. In spite of this triumph of democracy, more than half of the world continues to be underrepresented. Women's voices are still faint in the halls of world government.

This book endeavors to answer, through an interdisciplinary analysis of the Scandinavian political system, the following questions concerning female political leadership:

1. Is there a female style of nonaggressive leadership that relies on a power-sharing strategy rather than a power-wielding one?
2. Does this style apply only to women?
3. Would women leaders promote peace and social justice better than their male counterparts have done in the past?

The book begins by establishing a rigorous theoretical baseline on gender equality and/or differences; then the focus turns to women in power. Specifically, I use the Scandinavian political system as a case study. The Nordic countries have gained worldwide recognition for their gender equality. Norway, Iceland, Sweden, Denmark, and Finland have developed an impressive record in regard to putting women in positions of political leadership, at both the executive and legislative level. The hope is that lessons can be learned from the Scandinavian political system. The book also provides a case study analysis of two Scandinavian female leaders and one from the developing world.

If it is true that women tend to encourage more socially just and peaceful societies than men do, then it follows that there should be some encouragement for women to run for office and for people to elect them. If it is the style of leadership that is more important, then men could learn the characteristics that women exhibit and use them to develop greater social justice and peace in the world.

EQUALITY-DIFFERENCE DEBATE

Although few women have been national leaders, probably more have than most people think (see the Appendix). However, very little attention has been paid to these women leaders. Given the terrible crises we face at this point in history (i.e., ethnic conflict, environmental degradation, proliferation of weapons of mass destruction), it is worthwhile to ask if female leadership or female-style leadership could provide some guidance. The underlying thesis for this book is, Can an empowering, cooperative approach to leadership (usually attributed to women) develop and encourage social justice and peace?[1] This cooperative approach is not exclusively a female domain, nor do all women subscribe to it. However, women appear to have been on the forefront of this kind of leadership style. Women's traditional roles, socialized as nurturers and sustainers of life, may have prepared them for the role of empowering, cooperative leadership. Because of women's lack of political power, this leadership style has been ignored, whether it has been employed by women or men. It seems logical to assume that in order to break free from the Cold War mentality of militarization, the hierarchical, dominating leadership style of the past must be changed. History has shown that imperialist domination—one group believing itself to be superior to another through race, ethnicity, sex, religion, or culture—results in violence in all its forms.[2]

The clash of old and new ways of thinking about leadership was illustrated in a 1994 article in the *Seattle Times*. U.S. senator Phil Gramm (R-Texas) criticized U.S. attorney general Janet Reno, saying that, "she is a very sweet lady," but should not be attorney general because she cares more about day care than about violent crime. Senator Gramm continued: "I believe some people should have that priority, but I do not believe they should be attorney general of the United States." Reno has never said that child care is more important than prosecuting violent criminals, but she has said that one root cause of crime is the lack of day care and other social services to low-income children.[3]

Why should we be concerned with women in political power? Three reasons come to mind. First, in order to legitimate the democratic system, all citizens should be adequately represented. In the United States, although women are in the majority, only 9 percent of all national leaders are women. Second, if countries are drawing their leaders from only half of the eligible pool (men), it stands to reason that many quality leaders remain undiscovered. Third, women may bring into office some experiences and skills that men either have been lacking, or do not possess.

Examining feminist theory, one finds that there is not a monolithic stand on gender differences and/or equality. Feminist theorists do not agree on whether or not men and women are generally the same in their approach to national leadership. Because the body of literature on women national leaders is not large, there are few rigorous theoretical baselines to build on.[4] It is important to begin by defining three key terms: power, leadership, and social justice.

The concept of power has been studied incessantly by political scientists. Almost all international relations theorists (mainly men) have defined power. Nicholas J. Spykman described power as the "ability to move the individual or human collectivity in some desired fashion, through persuasion, purchase, barter, and coercion." Hans J. Morgenthau defined power as "man's control over the minds and actions of other men." Charles P. Kindleberger defined power as "strength plus the capacity to use it effectively in support of some objective."[5] To summarize the most common definitions, power is the ability to do or act; the capability of doing or accomplishing something; strength, might, force; the possession of control or command over others; authority; ascendancy; and one who possesses or exercises influence. Power is neither good nor bad; it is neutral. However, the characteristics that power brings to mind are usually masculine, often tinged with psychosexual connotations: strength, force, and authority over others.[6] Henry Kissinger's telling remark that "power is the ultimate aphrodisiac," illustrates this point.[7]

Traditionally, women have not been considered in the concept of power, and female use of power was considered illegitimate.[8] Traditional feminine traits have been excluded from the characteristics of power—society has defined power as being tough. Women themselves have been uncomfortable using power under these terms.[9] "Empowerment," on the other hand, is a concept that treats power as an expandable resource that is produced and shared through interaction of leaders and followers. Power then becomes an energy that transforms the leaders and followers—an effective leader is one who empowers others to act in their own interests.[10] This concept of empowerment emerged from feminist criticism of androcentric models of power.

Gender factors play into the conception and construction of power because men and women do not have the same access to resources that are associated with power and because they are socialized to use power differently. Do women actually use power differently than men do? Some feminist theorists argue that women define power as empowerment or "power to," while men see power as domination or "power over."[11] The traditional male "power over" concept captures only the ability to act or compel actions, whereas the female "power to" concept includes the power both to act and to refrain from action. These two concepts can best be understood through zero-sum/non-zero-sum game theory. "Power over" suggests a clear winner and loser. "Power to" allows for two winners. In other words, one person's gain is not necessarily another person's loss. Therefore, by using empowerment women can gain power without calling for the subordination of men.[12] When this book turns to the analysis of specific women leaders, empowerment can be tested for applicability at the national and international level.

Empowerment, popularly conceived as a female model of power, is a shared or cooperative effort as opposed to the domination game of male power. The female model is considered by feminist theorists to be better than the male model because it is more humane and less destructive. However, critics of this conception of female empowerment say that it is not exclusively female. Many men have promoted the empowerment notion of power (e.g., philosopher Michel Foucault). It was also popular with the New Left in the 1960s, whose commitment to feminism was somewhat questionable. For the sake of clarification, the women's movement may not have been the first to promote this view on power, but it seems to be the strongest voice now.[13] Another valid criticism of empowerment is that since power is seldom relinquished voluntarily, forceful means may be necessary to unseat those opposed to empowerment. Therefore, one might have to use the "power over" approach in order to institute the "power to" approach. This would, of course, be self-defeating.

The relationship between the mothering person (could be male) and the child also yields a new view of power. We are accustomed to thinking of power as something that can be wielded by one person over another, a means by which one person can bend another to his or her will. An ideal has been to equalize power so that agreements can be forged and conflicts defused. The superior power of the mothering person is relatively useless for most of what he or she aims to achieve in bringing up a child.

The mothering person seeks to empower the child to act responsibly; he/she neither wants to wield power nor to defend himself/herself against the power wielded by the child ... the mothering person's stance is characteristically one of caring, of being vulnerable to the needs and pains of the child, and of fearing the loss of the child before the child is ready for independence.[14]

Maternal thinking emerges from mothering and runs counter to militarism. Maternal thinking could give rise to cultural norms and practices very different from those that prevail in patriarchal society. The connection between mother's peacemaking and the nonviolence promoted by Gandhi and Martin Luther King, Jr., is clear. Many feminists believe that it is not female biology or anatomy that gives rise to the nonviolence of mothers but engagement in the activity of caring for, and raising, children (something men can also do if they have the opportunity or desire to).[15]

The term "leadership" has two general definitions:

1. a process of moving a group or groups of people in some direction through mostly noncoercive means, and
2. a process involving people in roles where guidance or direction of others is expected.

The second definition is more common. To move beyond the mind-set that has stagnated the concept of leadership, people must not be trapped by the second definition, which deals only with position. It is more important to look at the motivations and expectations of leaders and their followers and to deal with the process itself. Historian James MacGregor Burns developed an idea of "transforming leadership" where leaders are aware of the higher motivations and aspirations of their followers and build on those strengths. The objective is to go beyond power and include mutual needs, aspirations, and values. By turning followers into leaders, the transformational leader becomes a better leader.[16] Leadership in this study is defined as something that manifests itself through activity aimed at bringing about change in an organization or institution or social system in order to improve people's lives. The term "management" is often used interchangeably with leadership, but it is different. While to manage is to ensure that the system functions at its optimum level, leadership is a creative and innovative process that results in positive change.[17]

Having examined power and leadership, the term "social justice" remains to be defined. "Social" simply means having to do with humans living together, having to do with society or gregariousness. "Justice," on the other hand, is a more slippery term. It has been defined as righteousness, fairness, rightfulness, a reward or penalty as deserved, the use of authority to uphold what is just, or the administration of law. The term "justice" can be broken down into two distinctly different definitions:

1. a sense of fairness and
2. the authority to enforce that fairness.

Throughout history there has been a struggle to define what is just, fair, and rightful. These interpretations have been subjective and have changed over time. Historically, the dominant authority (usually determined by race, ethnicity, religion, culture, sex) has dictated what was fair. This is reflective of the hierarchical definition of human leadership—domination over others using power as opposed to sharing power or empowering others. To achieve optimum social justice or fairness in human society, empowerment may be the best course. As people come to realize their interdependence, they see power not as an individual asset but as an energy that must be shared.

Women are said to be underrepresented in positions of political leadership because of political socialization, situational/structural factors, and discrimination. But is it also because men are different from women? Some scholars argue that there are more differences *among* the sexes than *between* them (individual differences are more important than gender). With the rebirth of the American women's movement in the 1960s, the issue of differences between the sexes was raised. The U.S. media tended to characterize women as delicate, fragile, passive, and dependent. Men were portrayed as strong, rugged, active, intellectual, and independent. Many people thought that if women became like men, the very structure of society would crumble. This fear was based on the Western philosophical tradition that has defined women by their sexual, procreative, and childbearing functions.[18]

Perhaps societies, thereby our political structure, could be understood better using a family analogy rather than game theory (which has been the popular analogy during the Cold War). Martin Luther King, Jr., expressed this idea in an essay in which he wrote: "We live in a world house, a family unduly separated in ideas, culture, and interest, who, because we can never again live apart, must learn to live with each other in peace."[19] Gandhi, one of King's mentors, also saw the world as a family. Despite this sage advice, there is a tendency to follow hierarchical leaders. It could be that people's lives are complicated enough and that adding political decisions to the mixture causes overload, which can lead to apathy. Hierarchical leaders flourish in societies that are passive and noncontributory.[20]

Feminist theorists have noted that male dominance in society has been sustained through sexual stereotyping and social conditioning.[21] In response, feminists in the 1960s sought to add a female voice to the past—the assumption was that the female voice was different from the male's. Other feminists argued that noting differences between men and women would hinder the drive toward sexual equality, but is it really an "either-or proposition"? Is it really equality or difference?[22]

Feminist theorists can be categorized into three general groups:

1. those arguing that women's differences from men should be minimized (the equality position),
2. those holding that women are essentially different from men (essentialist position),[23] and
3. those who argue that because language is socially constructed, no categories of women are natural or inevitable, and such categorizations must be resisted (poststructuralist position).

The "equality versus difference" debate has been used as a quick way of characterizing the conflicting feminist positions and political strategies. The equality position holds that women and men are the same except for their anatomical differences. The difference position holds that women are psychologically and socially different from men. The "difference dilemma" emerged from this debate. Ignoring difference in the case of subordinated groups leaves a flawed neutrality in place. Focusing on difference can underscore the stigma of deviance. Focusing on, or ignoring, difference risks creating it.

Perhaps it is best to begin with an obvious observation, as children so very often do: women are not men, and men are not women. Most people would agree. In going further, however, difficulty arises—why do people believe women to be different from men? Beyond the biological difference, some theorists point out that people themselves produce and construct differences (psychologically, socially, and culturally) between men and women. According to this view, gender differences are created and are not permanent. How did these differences come to be? This is especially important as it relates to the question of gender inequality in society. It follows, then, that these differences do not necessarily have to be accepted as a given.[24]

The concept of poststructuralism (or postmodernism) holds that knowledge is grounded in language that does not reflect reality. Language creates a world that is not definitive but always in transition. The woman-as-peacemaker role, then, may be a distortion of reality that serves only to perpetuate the existing patriarchy. The dilemma for women is that few will listen to them if they do not speak the language of power (male power)— yet the process of learning the language forces them to leave their own identities behind. This is also true for men who do not speak the language of power. The objective for women seeking power should be to first learn the language, then deconstruct it.[25] It is common to think of language as merely a tool or a mirror of reality. Once designations of things enter the language, people are constrained by them. Language constructs reality through personal intercommunication. Since men have controlled lan-

guage throughout history, it is no wonder that men have dominated.

A lot of weight has been given to postmodernism. Researcher Virginia Held proposes that

[p]ost-structuralist and postmodernist critiques have illuminated feminist analyses of philosophical positions shown to reflect a more Western perspective rather than a universal one, and have been followed by
postmodern rejections of any totaling claims about women or about
what women essentially are.[26]

Author Catharine Stimpson in her book *Where the Meanings
Are* accepts postmodern fragmentation and holds we should not
try to achieve unified views. Accordingly, we should live culturally and politically with fragmentation.[27] The problem with
postmodernism, according to Held, is that it may undermine
feminist ideas. The postmodernist suggestion that there is no
category "woman" and that no general claims about women are
justifiable may go as far as to render women unable to demand
an end to subordination or even construct theories.[28]

Researcher Jane Flax believes that three kinds of thinking
have best represented our times: psychoanalysis, feminist theory,
and postmodern philosophy. Postmodern discourses are all "de-
constructive" in that they seek to distance us from, and make us
skeptical about, beliefs concerning truth, knowledge, power, the
self, and language that are often taken for granted within, and
serve as legitimization of, contemporary Western culture.[29]

Feminist theories, like other forms of postmodernism, should
encourage us to tolerate and interpret ambivalence, ambiguity,
and multiplicity as well as to expose the roots of our needs for
imposing order and structure no matter how arbitrary and op-
pressive these needs may be. If we do our work well, "reality"
will appear even more unstable, complex, and disorderly than it
does now.[30]

Deconstruction is one of two recent postmodernist movements. The other is constructivism. Both assert that meanings are
historically bounded and constructed through language. Constructivism holds that reality is not discovered; it is invented.
Human beings do not sit passively and observe reality; they build

it. From a constructivist standpoint, the real nature of male and female cannot be determined. For example, how much difference is significant? The anatomical differences between men and women seem slight when humans are compared to flowers or birds. The origins of differences may be largely social and cultural. One can therefore assume that these differences are fluid.[31]

Deconstructionism denies that there is a single, fixed meaning. It began as a literary technique that determined how the meaning of one word depends on its relation to other words—how one word is different from other words. For example, "female" is partly defined as "not male." Using the two poststructural or postmodernist perspectives, there appears to be no correct view of gender.[32]

Feminist theorist Joan Scott used a deconstructionist approach when she wrote that deconstruction is

an important exercise, for it allows us to be critical of the way in which ideas we want to use are ordinarily expressed, exhibited in patterns of meaning that may undercut the ends we seek to attain. A case in point—of meaning expressed in a politically self-defeating way—is the "equality-versus-difference" debate among feminists. Here a binary opposition has been created to offer a choice to feminists, of either endorsing "equality" or its presumed antithesis "difference." In fact, the antithesis itself hides the interdependence of the two terms, for equality is not the elimination of difference, and difference does not preclude equality.[33]

Scott further suggests that "instead of remaining within the terms of existing political discourse, we need to subject those terms to critical examination. Until we understand how the concepts work to constrain and construct specific meanings, we cannot make them work for us." She concludes that "equality requires the recognition and inclusion of differences." It is possible to promote the special attributes of women and stress the interdependence of the sexes. Acknowledging differences, if it leads to a partnership of cooperation through diversity, can be beneficial for society.[34]

In Western culture women and men are said to use power differently. When women do use power differently, there are negative consequences.[35] Women are thought to rely on softer emotions and persuasion, whereas men rely on aggressiveness. Women in many cultures lack the legitimate power of authority, yet many exercise power behind the scenes. Since values are so crucial in one's leadership style, it would make sense that differences in values would affect leadership. Values that appear to be held by more women than men—feminist values—would, then, lead to a different style of leadership.[36]

In a psychological study evaluating male and female leaders, men and women were asked to perform similar leadership tasks. Although the tasks were identical, women were perceived differently than men. There was an indication of a clear bias to evaluate women less favorably than men. It follows, then, that women will be perceived as using power differently as well.[37] Studies have shown that women tend to exhibit a more interactive style of leadership. They encourage participation, share power and information, and enhance other people's self-worth. Women enter politics to solve problems; men enter to gain power. Women tend to be better listeners than men. All of these attributes characterize women's style of leadership. It should be noted that men can also exhibit these tendencies—granted, perhaps fewer men than women. A balancing of engendered characteristics may be the best solution.[38]

Are women who take an active interest in diplomatic affairs predisposed by their socialization as females in American society to favor peaceful, negotiated, rather than bellicose, military, solutions to international problems? The traditional stereotype of women as pacifists fits only some women. Many women who hold official positions do not have pacifist agendas. One of the many reasons for this may be the connections that got them to such positions, usually male connections, and male ideology.[39] Women must oppose war in intellectual as well as emotional and personal ways if their distinctly female approach (however socially conditioned it may be) to world affairs is to be effective. "Otherwise," according to historian Joan Hoff Wilson, "to talk about 'global feminism' as a countervailing force in the decisions governing relations between nations is to distort the decision-making process and to delude ourselves about the effectiveness of gender-gap politics."[40]

The great power of Marxist interpretation, according to feminist researcher Linda Kerber, was that it not only described a separation of spheres but also offered an explanation of the way in which that separation served the interests of the dominant classes. Separate spheres were due neither to cultural accident nor to biological determinism. They were social constructions camouflaging social and economic service, a service whose benefits were unequally shared.[41] The metaphor of men's and women's separate worlds remains resonant because it retains some superficial vitality (e.g., John Gray's book *Men Are from Mars, Women Are from Venus*). For all of our overlapping areas between men and women, vast areas of our experience and our consciousness do not overlap. The boundaries may be fuzzier than they once were, but our world is still very gendered. The reconstruction of gender relations is one of the most compelling social tasks. This reconstruction is related to major social questions: the feminization of poverty, equal access to education and profession, relations of power and abuses of power in public sector and in the family.[42]

Early studies of differences between men and women were based on unexamined stereotypes and sloppy research. Some theorists have postulated that many of the most salient differences between men and women were social constructs rather than natural phenomena and that one of the tasks of a nonsexist political scientist would be to analyze their sources and their implications for politics.[43]

The story of Jeanette Rankin comes to mind. Rankin was the first woman to serve in the U.S. Congress. Joining the Congress in 1916, she quickly made her name known when they voted on entry into World War I.[44] Her "no" vote was duly recorded. Many women suffragists complained that Rankin's "no" vote would set back the women's movement. Many men said that her vote was typical for a woman, not willing to fight for democracy. In other words, you cannot trust a woman to be a leader. This attitude toward women persists despite historical precedence for it not to. We can look back to Plato in Book V of *The Republic* to find that he thought differences between men and women were not relevant to their political capacities.

Another interesting theory is that women as leaders practice politics of connectedness that is rooted in the gender division of labor, that is, that women are the caregivers. Some sociobiologists claim differences are genetic-hormonal differences. Others claim that women's experiences as caregivers and mothers and men's experiences outside the home cause them to act differently. With this strict division, neither the man nor the woman is complete. Neither is then capable of functioning both as responsible citizen/leader and nurturer.[45] According to difference theorists, by more women becoming political leaders, more nurturing would occur in the public arena and would make politics more like women's work of love and caring.[46]

Looking ahead, Beverly A. Forbes, originator of the Theory F Transformational Leadership Model, holds that feminist values (e.g., empathy, nurturing, empowering others, peace, equality, interdependence) are more congruent with the leadership needs of the future than are traditional patriarchal values. She also notes that feminist values are chosen and can be chosen by men as well, that leadership styles are gender-related, not gender-specific, and that in the twenty-first century gender differences will be transcended, with the focus being on our common humanity.[47]

By calling differences between men and women irrelevant, the legal institution's framework fits more into categories constructed from the points of view of men. The concept of equality, as it has been developed in the law, has itself been enmeshed in the very gender system feminists are trying to overcome. Differences between men and women need to be recognized, not denied. For example, men do not become pregnant. It is only from the male point of view that pregnancy may seem to be best thought of as a "disability" similar to something males experience. What makes pregnancy a disability rather than an ability is the structure of work, not reproduction. We need theory that appreciates the differences without devaluing them.[48]

Difference may give women advantages. Women may have advantages in terms of organizing society so as not to destroy itself. In linguistic studies between boys and girls, differences point to separate linguistic cultures. Women are more commonly concerned with intimacy, network connections, negotiating, and relationships than are men. Men are commonly independent, asserting their status, and concern themselves with the avoidance of being put down in a hierarchical, competitive social world. Feminists are increasingly asserting that differences are often real and should be respected, not ignored. Principles of liberty and equality tested by feminist theorists have revealed their male-dominant tinge. Reconstruction of this principle is a genuine concern for increased equal freedom.[49]

Studies support the hypothesis that women and girls are everywhere more motivated to take care of infants and children than are men and boys, not because of any "maternal instinct," but because the sexual division of labor always places women and girls in the contact condition and men and boys in the no-contact condition. This is contrary to the notion that men are aggressive because they are poisoned by testosterone and woman are maternal because of their hormones.[50]

No matter what subtle biological differences there may someday prove to be between men and women on the average, those differences will never justify the sexual inequality that has, for centuries, been a feature of human social life.[51] This inequality, also known as androcentrism, is the privilege of male experience and the marginalization of female experience. Male experience is then the standard, and female experience is the deviation from the standard.[52]

In the difference/equality debate, those theorists who supported differences between genders came into their own in the 1980s. These difference theorists developed a critique of masculinity. Most woman-centered theorists see woman's special virtue as her ability to easily transcend the many isolated units and artificial polarities that men are said to almost compulsively invent. Women grow through relationships rather than artificially dichotomized independence. Women see a world that comprises relationships. According to theorist Sandra Bem:

Had women been the ones with the power to construct the dominant cultural institutions, it thus follows from the woman-centered perspective that we human beings would now be in much less danger of destroying ourselves and our planet than we are.[53]

Accordingly, the problem with men and their institution is that they are too concerned with separation, domination, and hierarchy and not concerned enough with connectedness, mutual empowerment, and harmony.

Taking a social-psychological perspective on male-female difference, what shapes men's and women's differing constructions of reality and their differing positions in society, the caregiving role in the division of labor or the experience of being subordinated, which creates an oppositional consciousness? We should not focus on patriarchy or women as victims or androgyny, which makes women invisible. Men should not be denigrated in the process of looking at these issues. Differences are socially constructed, we are all very diverse, and there are no "real men" or "real women."[54]

As guilty as the woman-centered discourse may thus have been of reproducing biological essentialism and especially gender polarization, its indirect critique of cultural androcentrism has been wonderfully illuminating.[55] Gender polarization is the organizing of social life around the male-female distinction. To dismantle this, we are left only with biological differences related to reproduction. Human psyche is simultaneously and inextricably both rational and emotional.[56]

WOMEN AND POWER

To say that women use power differently than men do may run into an essentialist argument (or the difference side of the equality-difference debate). The essentialist position on women assumes their identity to be independent of their environment. Essentialists presume that women possess a superior morality that they could apply to the political world. For example, the so-called gender gap in attitudes toward militarism is attributed to women's peaceful nature. Women's caring, maternal nature is said to be responsible for their great support for social welfare issues. Carol Gilligan argues that women have a "different [moral] voice" based on a female way of thinking:

In the different voice of women lies the truth of an ethic of care, of the tie between relationship and responsibility, and the origins of aggression in the failure of connection. The failure to see the different reality of women's lives and to hear the differences in their voices stems in part from the assumption that there is a single mode of social experience and interpretation.[57]

Carol Gilligan's work, which describes "an ethic of care," has been cited frequently as proof of the essence of a "woman's morality." Gilligan herself has asserted that she does not regard the ethic of care as a category of gender difference. Nonetheless, her work is widely understood as showing that women are different from men. This ethic of care is not exclusively female territory.[58]

An ethic of care could be an important intellectual concern for feminists; the debate around this concern should be centered not in discussions of gender difference but in discourse about the ethic adequacy as a moral theory. Joan C. Tronto believes the equation of care with female is questionable because the evidence to support the link between gender difference and different moral perspectives is inadequate. She also believes that to point out gender differences in a society where male is considered normal implies that female is inferior and that it may be philosophically stultifying because so much effort will be put into defending women's morality rather than exploring the ethic of care.[59]

By suggesting that the ethic of care is gender-related, Gilligan precludes the possibility that care is an ethic created in modern society by the condition of subordination.[60] Other researchers have noted that those who feel separated from others, such as men, tend to voice a morality of justice and that those who view themselves as connected, such as women, tend to express a morality of care. However, Gilligan does allow for a dual explanation of this difference. She suggests that whatever psychological dimension there might be to explain women's moral differences, there may also be a social cause: women's different moral expression might be a function of their subordinate or tentative social position.[61]

Successful advocacy of an ethic of care requires the exploration of a social and political theory that is compatible with the broadest levels of care. Proponents of an ethic of care must specify which social and political institutions they understand to be the context for moral actors. "It should give us pause that some of the most compelling visions of polities of care are utopian."[62]

Feminists should no longer celebrate an ethic of care as a factor of gender difference that points to women's superiority. They must now begin the task of constructing a full theory of care.

Whether the evidence found on causes of gender difference in morality is a psychological artifact of femininity, a cultural product of caretaking activity, or a positional result of social subordination, it is difficult to imagine how any of these causes or some combination of them could affect all individuals equally.[63]

However, it may be a mistake to assume that women's political consciousness is influenced only by their concerns as mothers. It is also affected by other aspects that are not rooted in the family or childbearing.[64] The danger is that uniqueness of women may cause antifeminism. Feminist theorist Mary Poovey suggests that women share a situational similarity that masquerades as a natural likeness. She worries that it threatens to mask differences driven by class and race.[65] It may also be risky to suggest the existence of gender-based differences in power behavior when evidence, although inconclusive, tends to suggest otherwise.

Among feminist theorists there is by no means consensus on such apparently elementary questions as: What is gender? How is it related to anatomical sexual differences? How are gender relations constituted and sustained? How do gender relations relate to other sorts of social relations such as class or race? What causes gender relations to change over time? Are there only two genders? Is there anything distinctively male or female in modes of thought and social relations? If there is, are these distinctions innate and/or socially constituted?[66]

It is also the case that physically male and female humans resemble each other in many more ways than we differ. Our similarities are even more striking if we compare humans to, say, toads or trees. So why ought the anatomical differences between male and female humans assume such significance in our sense of our selves as persons? Why ought such complex human social meanings and structures be based on, or justified by, a relatively narrow range of anatomical differences?[67]

The activities most associated with women—nurturing, mothering, and taking care of others—lead to women's minds being seen as reflecting the qualities of stereotypically female activities and their bodies. Even feminists sometimes say women reason and/or write differently and have different interests and motives than men do. Men are said to have more interest in utilizing the power of abstract reason, to want mastery over nature, and to be aggressive and militaristic.[68] Unless we see gender as a social relationship, rather than as an opposition of inherently different beings, we will not be able to identify the varieties and limitations of different women's or men's powers and the oppression of certain segments within particular societies.[69]

Do these findings and theories about women and men hold up when applied to the world of politics? As an example, in the United States 10 percent of all elected offices are held by women. While nearly all men in elected positions have backgrounds in law or business, 47 percent of elected women have backgrounds in teaching, social work, or secretarial or homemaker service. It seems reasonable to assume that people with different backgrounds, whether they are men or women, would probably develop different approaches. Moreover, women in politics tend to be stereotyped as naive (especially in matters of defense and finance), honest, incorruptible peacemakers. They are also seen as not loyal and unwilling to go along with, or play by, the rules of the game. Seen as moral gatekeepers, women are often left out of the inner power circle. Because there are so few women in top leadership positions, they lack the well-established support systems that men enjoy. They are therefore isolated in

the political world. They seem to be treading on paths they have
not been adequately socialized to walk.[70] However, a study indicates that the level of women's political participation might increase as a result of efforts to resocialize their orientations toward power.[71] According to one theorist:

Women's greatest contributions will be made not only when more of
them are involved, but when they understand the problems that power
creates for women in this society, determine to work with those problems and grow beyond them, and commit themselves to using their
strengths, both as discrete individuals and as women, to change the way
things are done.[72]

Most studies that have examined gender differences in personality traits of leaders do not see significant differences. Any
reported differences appear to occur in the perceptions of the
subordinates to female leaders, so the discrimination that women
feel could be due both to their style of leadership and to their
gender.[73] Men who exhibit so-called female styles of leadership
are often criticized and kept from progressing. Past attempts to
differentiate male and female traits in leadership have resulted in
women's being seen as ineffective leaders lacking in traditional
leadership characteristics.

What many theorists fail to note are the differences within
the gender. Partnerships of men and women could maybe bridge
the gap of understanding. Women's experiences as members of
primary groups, families, circles of friends, networks, and neigh-
borhoods could reconceptualize politics as the study not of
power but of communities in action.[74] One theorist suggests that

[i]nstead of a society determined by violent conflict modified by the
authority and restraints of law and preoccupied with economic gain, we
might have a society which saw as its most important task the flour-
ishing of children and the creation of human relationships worthy of the
aspirations of the children who will become women as well as men.[75]

Another theorist adds:

To replace the order of male domination with gender equality would be
certainly more fundamental than replacing the order of feudalism with

democratic institutions. There can be little doubt that movement toward the latter has had profound effects on a society's place in the world; movement toward the former is no doubt doing so now.[76]

Based on Thomas Kuhn's idea on fundamental change in scientific paradigms, feminists have identified certain anomalies in the current dominant paradigm on gender and leadership:

1. few women have been in leadership roles,
2. the "great man theory" of management dictates that women are too emotional, too suggestible, and too indecisive to lead, and
3. subordinates react differently to male and female leaders' exhibiting the same behaviors.[77]

In order for a paradigm shift to occur, these anomalies will have to be overcome. Since more women are coming into positions of political power, the first anomaly may be removed soon. It will take more time to overcome the second and third anomalies. Perhaps as more women become leaders, these old, negative stereotypes will fade away. Both men and women can practice an empowering, cooperative style of leadership, but it seems to be more common now for women to spur the effort to transform leadership because of their social conditioning and history of political subordination. A new gender-partnership style of leading may eventually emerge.[78]

The purpose of this study is to discover whether women make a difference when given a chance to lead. Since men have been dominating the world, and world peace seems elusive, is there reason to believe that women can do a better job than men have? It is perhaps most important to recognize that violence is pathological, not normal. People can be peaceful, and there is no need go on an extremist crusade to rid the world of men. All people in modern society have been socialized in violence and are taught to think that counterviolence is the only response to violence. This violence is often directed at women. One look at hard-core pornography reveals this.

But what can be done to change this socialization process of violence? A key to this problem may lie in the studies of some theorists who have postulated that people participating in wars are driven by obedience to authority, not aggression. This is key to changing the power structure. Well-known experiments by Robert Milgram have shown that people, with no apparent signs of aggressiveness, would do harm to others if ordered to do so.[79] This urgently points out the need to change the hierarchical, intimidation style of leadership where people blindly follow orders. In order to bring peaceful social change, nonviolence is the only solution. The cycle of violence must be broken. Men and women can use their socialized differences through a new partnership to strengthen the whole of society. There can be a sense of cooperation through diversity.[80]

Greater equality for women is conditioned by the degree to which a nation has a growing industrial base, the degree to which the reproductive and auxiliary home responsibilities are lifted off the shoulders of women, the degree to which both male and female social roles are redefined, and the degree to which a nationwide women's organization emerges and is recognized as a legitimate political force with institutionalized access to policy-making.[81]

The world outside of the mainstream Western one is changing, sometimes inperceptibly to others. In the Inupiat (Eskimo) culture of northern Alaska, women have slowly come into positions of power. There has not been any resistance from males within the Inupiat culture; it was seen as a natural progression. Perhaps this is a shift that has occurred many times throughout history.

In some non-Western, precolonial societies women were very involved in political activities. One such society was in Zambia. Not only did precolonial Zambian women have theoretical access to power and leadership, but some actually held power. This power was not confined merely to domestic or women's issues. While only a minority of Zambian women held such positions, women did exercise considerable power and influence policy. The legitimacy of women's participation was unquestioned. The colonial experience changed traditional Zambian society, and women were relegated to subordinate positions and not allowed to exercise political power.[82]

This author believes that there are some differences between men and women, but the differences between individuals are more important. Additionally, some differences are constructed. Being dragged down into a theoretical debate on differences and similarities that is highly charged in a political sense may not provide the answers that we are looking for. Perhaps by closely observing societies that have changed on their own, we can gain the necessary insight. This approach is the focus of the next chapter, an examination of the political culture of Scandinavia.

NOTES

1. Helen S. Astin and Carole Leland, *Women of Influence, Women of Vision: A Cross-Generational Study of Leaders and Social Change* (San Francisco, CA: Jossey-Bass Publishers, 1991), pp. xii-xiii. I refer to an approach to leadership that shares power through cooperative teamwork rather than wielding power through intimidation and hierarchy.

2. Violence can come in three basic forms: physical, cultural, and structural. See the works of Johann Galtung.

3. *Seattle Times*, 20 January 1994, A2.

4. The exception is the fine work in a recent anthology: Michael A. Genovese, ed., *Women as National Leaders* (London: Sage Publications, 1993). In the book the author attempts to develop a pretheory on gender and leadership issues.

5. James E. Dougherty, and Robert L. Pfaltzgraff, Jr., *Contending Theories of International Relations* (Philadelphia: Lippincott, 1971), pp. 84-85.

6. There has even been a hierarchy of power developed:
   1. coercion,
   2. authority,
   3. manipulation, and
   4. persuasion.

7. Nancy C. M. Harstock, "Prologue to a Feminist Critique of War and Politics," in Judith Hicks Stiehm, ed., *Women's Views of the Political World of Men* (Dobbs Ferry, NY: Transnational Publishers, 1984), p. 123.

8. Jane S. Jaquette, ed., *Women in Politics* (New York: Wiley, 1974), pp. 9-10.

9. Dorothy W. Cantor, Toni Bernay, and Jean Stoess, *Women in Power: The Secrets of Leadership* (New York: Houghton Mifflin, 1992), pp. 36-37.

10. Astin and Leland, pp. 1-2. See also Elizabeth Janeway, "Women and the Uses of Power," in Hester Eisenstein and Alice Jardine, eds., *The Future of Difference* (New Brunswick, NJ: Rutgers University Press, 1985), pp. 327-44; Sandra Morgen and Ann Bookman, eds., *Women and the Politics of Empowerment* (Philadephia, PA: Temple University Press, 1988), p. 4.

11. Iva Ellen Deutchman, "The Politics of Empowerment," *Women & Politics* 11, no. 2 (1991), 2-3.

12. Deutchman, p. 4.

13. Deutchman, pp. 6-11.

14. Virginia Held, *Feminist Morality: Transforming Culture, Society, and Politics* (Chicago: University of Chicago Press, 1993), p. 209.

15. Held, p. 152.

16. James MacGregor Burns, *Leadership* (New York: Harper & Row, 1978), p. 4.

17. Astin and Leland, pp. 4-5, 7.

18. Genovese, p. 2; Morgen and Bookman, p. 20; Francine D'Amico and Peter R. D'Amico, eds., *Women in World Politics: An Introduction* (Westport, CT: Bergin & Garvey, 1995), p. 3.

19. Martin Luther King, Jr., *Where Do We Go from Here? Chaos or Community* (New York: Harper & Row, 1967), pp. 1-2.

20. D'Amico and D'Amico, p. 4.

21. The concept of "separate but equal" overturned in 1954 by the Supreme Court in *Brown v. the Board of Education* comes to mind.

22. Hester Eisenstein and Alice Jardine, eds., *The Future of Difference* (New Brunswick, NJ: Rutgers University Press, 1985), pp. xv-xviii.

23. Peace researchers tend to point out the woman's traditional role as nurturer, and noncombatants.

24. Nancy Julia Chodrow, "Gender, Relation, and Difference," in Eisenstein and Jardine, *The Future of Difference*, pp. 3-19.

25. Linda Rennie Forcey, "Women as Peacemakers," *Peace & Change* 16, no. 4 (October 1991), 340-49.

26. Held, p. 13.

27. Catharine Stimpson. *Where the Meanings Are.* New York: Routledge, 1990; Held, p. 13.

28. Held, p. 13.

29. Jane Flax, "Postmodernism and Gender Relations in Feminist Theory," *Journal of Women in Culture and Society* 12, no. 4 (1987), 624.

30. Flax, p. 643.

31. Rachel T. Hare-Mustin and Jeanne Marecek, eds., *Making a Difference: Psychology and the Construction of Gender* (New Haven, CT: Yale University Press, 1990), pp. 455-56.

32. Hare-Mustin, pp. 460-46.

33. Joan Scott, "Deconstructing Equality-Versus-Difference: Or, the Uses of Poststructuralist Theory for Feminism," *Feminist Studies* 14, no. 1 (Spring 1988), 38.

34. Part of the problem with the equality-difference debate also involves the understanding of equality. Equality between the sexes has been measured by masculine standards. If men and women are to be equal, then women must be like men. If women insist on being women, then they cannot be equal. True equality will allow for differences. See Carole Pateman, "'Does Sex Matter to Democracy?'—A Comment," *Scandinavian Political Studies* 13, no. 1 (1990), 59; Scott, pp. 38, 39, 48; and Beverly A. Forbes, "Profile of the Leader of the Future: Origins, Premises, Values and Characteristics of the Theory F Transformational Leadership Model," Mimeograph (Seattle: University of Washington, 1991), pp. 19-21.

35. Paula Johnson, "Women and Power: Toward a Theory of Effectiveness," *Journal of Social Issues* 32, no. 3 (1976), 99-100.

36. Forbes, p. 18.

37. Hilary M. Lips, *Women, Men, & the Psychology of Power* (Englewood Cliffs, NJ: Prentice-Hall, 1981), pp. 54-58; Alice H. Eagly, Mona G. Makhijani, and Bruce G. Klonsky, "Gender and the Evaluation of Leaders: A Meta-Analysis," *Psychological Bulletin* 111, no. 1 (1992), 3.

38. Forbes, pp. 24-25.

39. Joan Hoff Wilson, "Conclusion: Of Mice and Men," in Edward P. Crapol, ed. *Women and American Foreign Policy: Lobbyists, Critics, and Insiders*. 2nd ed. (Wilmington, DE: Scholarly Resources, 1992), pp. 173-88.

40. Wilson, p. 185.

41. Linda K. Kerber, "Separate Spheres, Female Worlds, Woman's Place: The Rhetoric of Women's History," *Journal of American History* 75 (June 1988), 14.

42. Kerber, p. 39.

43. Martha Ackelsberg and Irene Diamond, "Gender and Political Life: New Directions in Political Science," in Beth B. Hess and Myra M. Ferree, eds., *Analyzing Gender: A Handbook of Social Science Research* (Newbury Park, CA: Sage Publications, 1987), p. 506.

44. She voted "no" to entry into World War II as well. So controversial was her vote that she had to be escorted by the police from the Capitol building after other members of Congress threatened her.

45. Ackelsberg and Diamond, pp. 509, 516.

46. Ackelsberg and Diamond, p. 517.

47. Forbes, pp. 5-6.

48. Held, pp. 165-66.

49. Held, p. 168.

50. Sandra L. Bem, *The Lenses of Gender: Transforming the Debate on Sexual Inequality* (New Haven, CT: Yale University Press), p. 37.

51. Bem, p. 38.

52. Bem, p. 41.

53. Bem, p. 148.

54. Bem, p. 138.

55. Bem, p. 132.

56. Bem, p. 192.

57. Carol Gilligan, *In a Different Voice: Psychological Theory and Women's Development* (Cambridge, MA: Harvard University Press, 1982), p. 173.

58. Joan C. Tronto, "Beyond Gender Difference to a Theory of Care," *Journal of Women in Culture and Society* 12, no. 4 (1987), 644-45.

59. Tronto, p. 646.

60. Tronto, pp. 646-47.

61. Tronto, pp. 648-49.

62. Tronto, p. 661.

63. Tronto, pp. 662-63.

64. Morgen and Bookman, pp. 20-22.

65. Deutchman, pp. 6-11.

66. Flax, p. 627.

67. Flax, p. 636.

68. Flax, p. 637.

69. Flax, p. 641.

70. Women are not always supportive of one another. They can have differing views that can lead to conflict.

71. Deutchman, p. 89.

72. Deutchman, p. 89.

73. Astin and Leland, p. 4.

74. Ackelsberg and Diamond, p. 28.

75. Held, p. 214.

76. Held, p. 216.

77. Astin and Leland, pp. 3-4.

78. Forbes, p. 17.

79. Annika Takala, "Feminist Perspectives on Peace Education," *Journal of Peace Research* 28, no. 2 (1991), 232-33.

80. Kathleen Maas Weigert, "Peace Studies as Education for Nonviolent Social Change," *Annals of the American Academy of Political and Social Science* 504 (July 1989), 40-41.

81. Margaret E. Leahy, *Development Strategies and the Status of Women* (Boulder, CO: Lynne Rienner, 1986), p. 117.

82. Isla Schuster, "Political Women: The Zambian Experience" in Marilyn Safir, Martha T. Mednick, Dafne Israell, and Jessie Bernard, eds., *Women's Worlds: From the New Scholarship* (New York: Praeger, 1985), pp. 189, 190, 196.

Chapter 2

Women's Rise to Power in Scandinavia

> Women must enter politics if they are to have an in-
> fluence on their lives.
> —Fernanda Nissen, 1901

COMPARATIVE HISTORY

The Nordic countries, comprising Norway, Denmark, Sweden, Finland, and Iceland, are small, homogeneous societies with relatively high standards of living, a fairly common historical tradition and culture, and emphasis on Protestantism, democracy, and social welfare. Slightly more than 20 million people live in the Nordic region or Scandinavia, ranging from 8 million in Sweden to only 200,000 in Iceland.[1] Danish, Norwegian, and Swedish are all very close languages and can be easily understood by citizens of those Nordic countries. Finnish and Icelandic people need to speak one of the other three Nordic languages to be understood throughout Scandinavia. All Nordic societies have low birthrates and high life expectancies, and the people are fairly stable, with a small percentage of them being either extremely poor or extremely wealthy.[2] During the twentieth century, the populations of the Nordic countries have become older. The care of the elderly, primarily women, is performed mostly by women.[3]

The postwar era brought economic expansion that shifted the economic base from that of fisheries and agriculture to industrial and service based sectors. By the 1970s economic conditions were fairly similar in all Nordic states, and women had emerged in politics. Although women entered rapidly into political life by the 1970s throughout Scandinavia, their position within the family and in the workplace did not progress as rapidly. The proportion of women in Nordic parliaments is high compared to world standards—women constitute between 33 and 39 percent of parliaments in four Nordic countries and 24 percent in Iceland. As impressive as these percentages are, the majority of decision-making bodies in the Nordic countries are still dominated by men. Additionally, women are underrepresented in private sector management in Scandinavia—only a few percent of the high-level positions are held by women.[4]

Progress in terms of more women attaining political power is partly due to the fact that women were better educated by the 1960s and 1970s. However, women tended to crowd into only a few areas of study. Also, the number of women working outside the home has increased dramatically. This is due to rapid economic expansion after World War II and the need for labor. The higher cost of living has led many women to seek a family's second income. Demographic factors, such as decline in marriage and birthrates and the rise in the incidence of divorce, have also contributed to more women being in the workplace. Public policy has supported the move of women into the workforce through expanded educational opportunities and child-care facilities.[5]

Men and women in Nordic societies perform the same amount of work, on average. But women perform more unpaid work. Gender roles emerge in families with children. Mothers perform the most unpaid work (housework and the care of one's own children). Between 50 and 80 percent of three-to six-year-old children in Nordic countries attend day care. Women as a group perform two-thirds of the total unpaid work. As a result, women have less time to spend on gainful employment, personal enrichment, and career development.[6]

Women are primarily employed in the service sector of Nordic economies, while men are fairly well distributed throughout all sectors. Although both men and women enjoy high levels of education in Scandinavia, women tend to dominate in medical fields, education, and the humanities, while men dominate in engineering, mathematics, and computer science fields. Men devote most of their time to their working life, whereas women divide their time between work and family. This has caused a gap between men's and women's incomes in Scandinavia.[7]

Women's political participation tends to be highest in social democratic societies—where the government's role is to equalize social and economic inequities. Conversely, women's political participation is not as acceptable or easy to build in cultures where individual rights are stressed above all.[8] Some regions of the world appear to be ahead of others in terms of women's involvement in politics. It stands to reason, then, that societies in such regions would be fertile test-beds for theories on female political leadership. Norway, Sweden, Iceland, Finland, and Denmark lead the world in terms of percentage of women in Parliament.[9] But how do women affect politics in the Nordic region?

In Scandinavia, women find that they are judged collectively by their peers. Most women politicians in Scandinavia want to make a difference, but they do not want to act too differently. They tend to avoid conflicts with their male counterparts and do not seriously challenge the party line. Despite increasing numbers of women in politics, they are still fearful of being singled out as women politicians. To more fully understand the systemic factors that led to such a high percentage of women political leadership in Scandinavia, we place particular emphasis on Norway's political system, a system that is representative of the Scandinavian political culture.

One of the first questions people ask in regard to the subject of women in power is, What difference do women make? What differences are there between male and female politicians in Norway that can be quantified? To answer this question, Norwegian members of Parliament were asked to name the political issues that were most important to them. These data are presented in Table 2.1 which suggests that male and female parliamentarians in Norway have very different interests. Some of these differences affirm the gender traits discussed earlier. One assumption that may be drawn from these data is that if men and women have such different interests in politics, then certainly their style of leadership would be quite different as well. But despite the increasing number of women in the political system in Norway, and despite the clear differences in interests, did these women provide enough change and influence to modify or replace the patriarchal system?[10]

In Norway, a strong belief in the political relevance of difference has helped provide access for women to top political posts. Conceptualizations of gender specificity and of difference have been internalized by men and women alike and currently provide clear descriptions of male and female worlds of political concern. But the categorical images projected throughout the gender rhetoric contain few guidelines to the actual behavior of women on elite levels of politics.

There are a number of reasons for Norway's success in promoting female leadership in politics (these hold for the rest of Scandinavia as well):

1.   a deep appreciation for democracy and equity,
2.   a well-organized women's movement,
3.   Lutheran religion,
4.   women who belong to left-wing or socialist parties,
5.   high education level for women,
6.   high percentage of women in the workforce,
7.   electoral system based on proportional representation, and
8.   party lists or ballots with many candidates.[11]

Table 2.1
Women's and Men's Political Interests in the Norwegian
Parliament, 1991

Policy Issue	Men %	Women %
Environmental Protection	0	26
Economic/Industrial	42	0
Social Welfare	0	25
Energy	21	0
Equality	0	24
Transportation	13	0
Disarmament	0	12
Education	0	7
National Security/ Foreign Affairs	12	0
Other	12	6

Source: Hege Skjeie. "The Rhetoric of Difference: On Women's Inclusion into Political Elites." *Politics & Society* 19, no. 2 (June 1991), 239.

Two revolutions have occurred in terms of women's rights in Norway. The first came in the 1960s and 1970s, when women entered the workforce in large numbers. In 1965 nine of ten Norwegian mothers worked only at home. In 1993, 72 percent worked outside the home. The other revolution has been the enormous growth of women's education. Today, women account for 52 percent of the total number of students enrolled at universities and colleges.[12]

Norway's multiple-party system creates greater consensus than the U.S. two-party system, which tends to produce more conflict than consensus. Class differences are not as pronounced in Norway, owing mainly to the fact that Norway was until recently a rather poor country. Some feminists in Norway trace the tradition of equity back to Viking times. Viking women needed more legal rights because the men were so often gone from home. Also, unlike other Nordic countries, Norway had experienced long periods of foreign domination—Denmark, Sweden, and Germany have all dominated Norway at one time. Norway is a relatively new nation. Norway lived under Danish rule for over 400 years, ending in 1814 with the drawing of its constitution. The country was then ceded to Sweden, which formed a union with Norway that lasted until 1905, when Norway finally became an independent nation. The Germans took over Norway from April 1940 until May 1945. Social democracy prevailed after the war, and the government saw itself as an agent of positive social change. This history of foreign domination has contributed to the Norwegians' strong sense of democracy and tendency to identify with the oppressed and underprivileged.[13]

THE NORDIC NEXUS

The strong cultural tradition of consensus seeking in Norway is partly based on a broader Nordic phenomenon. In the twentieth century, the modern Nordic states built their spirit of political consensus on the heritage of Scandinavianism. Scandinavianism began as a movement in the 1830s to develop closer ties and cooperation between Swedish and Danish leaders. The Scandinavianists combined ideas of a defense community, a union, and a dynastic confederation. Famous Norwegian literary figures like Bjørnstierne Bjørnson and Henrik Ibsen supported a Scandinavian union. The Russians took Scandinavianism seriously enough to consider it a security threat.[14]

The impact of social democracy on the political culture of Scandinavia must be taken into consideration as part of this consensus. The real base of Nordic cohesiveness—and the first element in what I call the Nordic nexus—is the spirit of political consensus inherent in the character of Nordic societies.[15]

Group behavior in modern Nordic societies is distinctive due to the following characteristics: the legitimacy, density, and centralization of groups and their systematic incorporation into the legislative and administrative process. Legitimacy means that the Nordic societies combine the supreme worth of the individual with the desirability of collectiveness. This has resulted in a very powerful social norm according to which everybody should belong to a group. The density of Nordic organizations is reflected in the fact that 90 percent of wage earners are union represented, as are 70 percent of white-collar workers. Centralization has more effectively utilized the scarce resources inherent to small countries.[16]

A comparison of Nordic and U.S. political cultures points to some interesting differences between the two societies. Nordic political culture is not individualistic as in the United States. Political thinking in the Nordic countries is not flamboyant. Nordic societies believe that aid to one sector of the community will provide benefits to the whole. This sense of interconnectedness has led to the formulation of a labor policy of continuously retraining workers, thus realizing the relationship between social justice and economic development. In summary, politics in Scandinavia are characterized by broad scope, political responsibility, competence, and continuous political education.[17]

The political culture and institutional structure in Scandinavia have tended to exhibit deferent values and accommodationist institutions. This is in contrast to the United States, where self-assertive values and adversarial institutions are pervasive. Nordic political culture is not overly burdened by the worries inherent in a legalistic, adversarial society. With the dominance of the Social Democratic Party since the 1930s, modern Nordic people have perpetuated the tradition of accommodation and deference.[18] Nordic-type deference is also directly opposed to the concept of rugged individualism that has been so pervasive in American culture.[19]

Social democracy emerged from this Nordic tradition of accommodation and deference. From their earliest origins, socialist parties throughout Northern Europe were closely related to working-class organizations, and together they constituted the labor movement. Through their ability to integrate and unite under common policy programs and objectives, the labor movements transformed their crucial role in the capitalist system into an effective political voice.[20]

Since the 1940s the new social democratic strategy has been to collaborate with nonsocialist forces and to build unity and integration of the labor movement with the aim of facilitating rapid expansion of economic resources in order to finance social reform.[21]

The Nordic people increased social justice in their societies while harnessing all of the advantages—and suffering none of the disadvantages—of the purely capitalist mode of production.[22] Social democratic ideology has combined welfare, egalitarianism, and economic control with the continued dominance of individual ownership—giving rise to the paradox some extremists on either end of the political-economic spectrum apparently see. Socialists describe the Nordic region as "capitalist," and capitalists describe it as "socialist."[23]

EQUAL OPPORTUNITY IN SCANDINAVIA

From an international perspective, the Nordic countries enjoy a high standard of living and are generally regarded as pioneers in terms of equal opportunity policies (please see Table 2.2). Key to this accomplishment is the fact that Nordic societies encourage men and women to combine their economic activities and parenthood. As evidence of this, Scandinavia has one of the world's highest labor force participation rates for men and women and the highest percentage of women in politics.[24] Long before it was popular in the United States, Scandinavian men shared household and childrearing duties with their spouses.

Table 2.2
Milestones for Equal Opportunity in Scandinavia

	Denmark	**Finland**	**Iceland**	**Norway**	**Sweden**
Suffrage	1915	1906	1915	1913	1921
First Woman in Parliament	1918	1907	1922	1922	1921
First Woman Cabinet Minister	1924	1926	1970	1945	1947
First Woman Prime Minister	N/A	N/A	N/A	1981	N/A

Source: Nordic Council of Ministers. *Women and Men in the Nordic Countries: Facts and Figures 1994*. Copenhagen, Denmark: Nord 1994:3, p. 14.

Women still bear the main responsibility for child-care, although men have begun to exercise their legal right to paid parental leave. This caregiver role seems to be an obstacle for women's achieving economic parity with men. To aid in promoting women and achieving equality, the Nordic countries entered into a formalized equal opportunity agreement in 1978. The goal for the cooperation is to strengthen the national equal opportunity efforts and to incorporate work with gender issues into all national policy fields, including the activities of the Nordic Council of Ministers. The plan for 1995-2000 concentrates on the following concerns:

1. to promote women's and men's equal access to political and economic decision processes
2. to promote equality in women's and men's economic positions and influence (activities to promote equal pay are an important part of this effort)
3. to promote a working life with equal opportunities

4. to improve the possibilities for both women and men to combine parenthood and economic activities
5. to influence European and international development in the sphere of equal opportunity[25]

In Denmark, the first legislation on equality—the Act on Equal Remuneration for Men and Women—was passed in 1976. Since that time, four more laws have been added:

1. The Act on Equal Opportunities for Women and Men of 1978.
2. The Act on Equal Treatment of Women and Men as Regards Access to Employment, Maternity leave, etc., of 1978.
3. The Act on Equality of Women and Men in Appointing Members of Public Committees etc., of 1985.
4. The Act on Equality of Women and Men in Appointing Certain Board Members of the Civil Service of 1990.

In Finland, the Act on Equality between Women and Men of 1987 placed responsibility for promoting equality on all public and private employers. There are additional requirements regarding education and teaching. The act also contains provisions prohibiting sex discrimination. The three goals of the act are to prevent sexual discrimination, promote equality between men and women, and improve the status of women, especially in their work life.

In Iceland in 1976, the Equal Rights Act came into force, replacing the Equal Pay Commission Act. It has been revised twice, once in 1985 and again in 1991. The act forbids sex discrimination but stipulates that temporary measures can be employed to improve women's status. Equality is ensured in education, employment, and wages. Labor unions and employers are required to take steps necessary to equalize the status of women in the labor market. There was also special emphasis on equalizing the makeup of official boards, committees, and councils.

The Equal Opportunities Act took effect in Norway in 1979. Public officials were charged with altering conditions within society to attain equality for women. Women and men were to be afforded the same opportunity to education and work. The act called for giving advantage to women in education admissions and occupational recruitment in the case of the male and female applicants having the same merits. Further refinements, namely, the Working Environment Act, require the workplace to be designed in such a way as to afford equal opportunity for both sexes. The law also extends rights to women for parental leave and shortened work hours to care for, and nurse, children.

In Sweden, the 1992 Equal Opportunity Act superseded initial 1980 legislation. Employers must promote a balance of gender in positions and make special efforts to attract applicants from underrepresented genders. Employers are required to be flexible with their employees who are parents and equalize pay between men and women who hold the same type of jobs. Sex discrimination is banned in hiring, the workplace, pay, choice of assignment, and termination. Employers with more than ten employees are required to file annual reports that detail equality plans and active measures taken to ensure workplace and hiring equality.[26]

POWER AND INFLUENCE IN POLITICS

Women in Norway ran for local office in 1901 and were elected. By 1913 Norwegian women were able to vote nationwide.[27] Table 2.3 details the progress of women's gaining elected office in Norway.

Norway never had a landowning aristocracy, a fact that may have contributed to its egalitarian attitudes. Norway still has what is called the "Janta" law. This is not a law at all but a social norm that says that one should never stick one's head up too much higher than others. "Do not believe that you are someone special," was advice offered to many Norwegians. Do not be too successful or too rich, in other words. Norwegians also have a national predisposition toward joining organizations. This increased the ability of women to organize effective vehicles for promoting their rights within society. Although Norwegian women won the right to vote comparatively early by interna-

tional standards, progress was slow for women to get into political office (as shown in Table 2.3). There was a debate over
woman suffrage that went on for some time in Norway, but by
1913 those opposed to women's voting simply ran out of arguments. An overwhelming majority, 80 percent, voted for women
to be enfranchised.

Table 2.3
Women's Representation in Norwegian Political Assemblies

Year	% Local	% County	% National	% Cabinet
1901	0.8	0.0	0.0	0.0
1945	3.4	na	5.0	7.0
1973	14.8	5.4	16.0	20.0
1981	22.8	28.8	26.0	24.0
1987	31.2	40.6	36.0	44.0
1991	28.5	38.6	36.0	47.0

Source: Marit Tovsen. "Women in Politics in Norway." Seminar paper for
Women from Eastern Europe, Denmark, 19 August 1992, mimeograph, 5.

Table 2.4 and Figure 2.1 illustrate the status of women in
political power throughout Scandinavia. One can see that the
percentages are very close.

The 1970s brought a change in that women voted differently;
they were concerned with women's issues. By the late 1960s and
early 1970s women composed still only 9.5 percent of the local
councils, 8 percent of the Parliament, and 7 percent of the cabinet. A key date was 1961, when an agreement was made to
equalize pay between men and women. In the 1967 campaign

women voters exercised their right to change the order of the party lists and put women candidates on top. This meant that when a certain party won a certain number of seats, the people on the top of the party list would get those elected seats. This list ordering had been done before to keep women off the top of the list; now it was reversed.

Table 2.4
Percentage of Women in Nordic Government Assemblies, 1994

	Parliament	County Councils	Municipal Councils
Denmark	34	29	26
Finland	39	na	30
Iceland	24	na	22
Norway	39	39	29
Sweden	33	43	34

Source: Nordic Council of Ministers. *Women and Men in the Nordic Countries: Facts and Figures 1994*. Copenhagen, Denmark: Nord 1994:3, p. 34.

In 1971 the women's organizations in Norway organized an effective national campaign that led to the placement of many more women on councils and Parliament, the so-called women's coup. Despite the complaining that ensued, women still represented only 15 percent of the elected positions after the coup.[28]

In the 1970s a number of issues surfaced affecting women. Almost all social inequities that existed were exposed and dealt with. Abortion rights were secured in 1978, and shorter hours for working mothers were demanded. The new women's organizations differed from those of the older generation in that they

worked both in and out of the political system raising the consciousness of women throughout the country with a feminist
counterculture. The culmination of all of these efforts was the
passage of the Equal Status Act in 1978.[29]

Figure 2.1
Percentage of Women in Nordic Parliaments, 1907-91

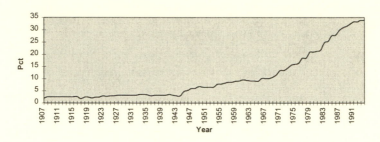

Source: Nordic Council of Ministers. *Women and Men in the Nordic Countries:
Facts and Figures 1994*. Copenhagen, Denmark: Nord 1994:3, pp. 72-73.

The Equal Status Act of 1978 had two aims. One, it was
passed to ensure substantive equality of treatment in most areas
between men and women. On the other hand, the act is also in-
tended to influence attitudes toward sex roles. The objective of
the act is to

promote equal status between the sexes and aims particularly at improving the position of women. The public authorities shall facilitate
equality of status between the sexes in all sectors of society. Women
and men shall be given equal opportunities for education, employment
and cultural and professional advancement.[30]

The 1980s were truly the decade of the woman in Norway.
Women dramatically increased their participation in all leadership positions throughout Norway, including the prime minister's
office, with the coming to power of Gro Harlem Brundtland.
Women represented over 30 percent of all elected offices after
the 1985 elections.[31]

In 1983 the Norwegian Labor Party decided to use the quota system to form their party lists. The 40 percent mark was chosen. This was considered a rather drastic measure to integrate women in politics. The use of quotas also helped increase the number of women in power. An addition to the Equal Status Act in 1988 stated that all public boards and committees should include at least 40 percent of each sex.[32] Another explanation for the disparity between so many women in politics and so few in positions of corporate leadership holds that women have filled in "shrinking institutions."

Some political theorists in Norway believe in the "shrinking institutions theory," which holds that women are being elected to public office because real power is being shifted to the private sector, where men still dominate. Many other theorists discount this theory.[33]

Norwegian researcher Hege Skjeie disputes the shrinking institutions theory and holds that the very foundation of the thesis is inadequate. The myth of shrinking institutions implies a new form of female powerlessness, according to Skjeie. It devalues the significance of women's struggle to gain full rights as citizens, and it implies that what they did get was given to them the easy way.[34]

Shrinking institutions theorists claimed that power shifts from the Parliament to the cabinet. But now that women make up a bigger percentage of the cabinet than in Parliament, it is hard to make that claim. Nevertheless, in 1991, when three of the leading political parties in Norway were headed by women, Norwegian newspapers asserted that "when power disappears, so do the men—politics are now being left to women." To illustrate this claim, the newspaper presented pictures of eleven prominent male politicians who now occupy positions at the top of state and private business hierarchies.[35]

The theory also points out that the political system in Norway is traditionally one of bargaining or corporate decision making. In the Norwegian context, bargaining is expressed institutionally through an elaborate system of public boards and commissions. This system provides one central arena for negotiations over the formulation of public policies and is still recognized as an important meeting place for political representatives, organizational leaders, civil servants, and those with legal and technical expertise. Women's weaker presence within most of these relevant strata of leadership has often been presented as preventing their access to corporate decision making.[36]

The Equal Status Act was designed primarily as a regulation covering working life. It granted women equal access to the labor market through the prohibition of discriminatory practices and addressed problems with wage distribution in segregated labor markets.[37]

By the 1980s, with so many women entering the labor market, a new emphasis emerged—that of child care and parental leave policies. From the mid-1980s on, political priorities shifted to public funding of parental leave and state subsidies to promote child-care centers. Most political parties acknowledged these new initiatives to be a direct result of women's increased participation in politics.[38]

From the 1970s the common concerns of womanhood were the primary motivation for women's participation in politics. Within feminist political science scholarship, a perspective that stressed gender-structured political interests was combined with an emphasis on political integration as a strategy of empowering women. Actual representation by women was necessary, it was felt, because men could not represent the interests or values of women.[39]

In Norway, there is a great tradition of social representation. Norway's Parliament, the Storting, reflects the composition of Norwegian society more faithfully than do most other parliaments. This type of "descriptive representation" closely links a candidate's experiences and background to the political views of the candidate. This has encouraged the rapid assimilation of the principle of women's integration. Today the political relevance of gender is shared by most Norwegian political groups. Men and women alike now conceptualize gender specificity and difference as being directly relevant to political decision making.[40]

The traditional Nordic passion for equality has served as the reference point for most efforts to explain what are relatively isolated cases. The Nordic countries are small and fairly homogeneous, and values of justice, equality, and solidarity are considered strong. Thus, the explanation goes, when women demanded political representation as a group, their claim received recognition and was regarded as legitimate by party leadership.[41]

Skjeie's point is that Norway's goal of balanced gender representation is close to being achieved. Women's integration in the political world is not just symbolic—an empty gesture granted by men who have moved to the real seats of power. There exists no convincing empirical basis for claims that women have inherited from men positions that are becoming less significant in terms of power and influence. The construction of a myth of women's integration into shrinking institutions only serves to devalue women's struggle to gain equal rights to political participation. The Norwegians have generally accepted the political relevance of gender. The arguments that emphasize difference have provided legitimacy to women's claims for representation as a group. From this basis, party competition has so far proved to be an effective mechanism of integration. When gender is acknowledged as a politically relevant issue, the fear of losing women voters helps standardize the representation profiles of the different parties.[42]

Norway's first female government in 1986 signified a shift of perspective. People began to focus on what changes women would make. The ideal of reaching the magical 50 percent representation mark should make some differences, according to many theorists. The underlying assumption is that women should represent women's interests.

Another issue that has emerged with the increasing number of women in office in Norway is that of principles of leadership. Should leaders be chosen for their representation or their competence? Gender has become the most important criterion for political nomination. But do women leaders see themselves as women's only representatives? Can representation and competence be balanced in politics? Representation can be measured by group association based on age, gender, residence, or by party affiliation. Competence is generally measured by political experience, education, and personal leadership attributes such as decisiveness, loyalty and tolerance, and creativity. Those who argue that women should not be let in just because they are women ignore the fact that if political experience is then the most important criterion, and few women are in positions of leadership, how will they ever get the experience unless they are afforded the opportunity? Once women are elected or appointed, then they will get experience and will either prove themselves competent or fail.[43]

When considering women as political leaders, one must also question leadership style. Political scientists have outlined two basic theories of representation:

1. the instructed delegate theory, and
2. the trustee theory.

Instructed delegates mirror the wishes of their constituents. Trustees act according to their own judgment in behalf of the interests of the citizens. The instructed delegate can also be thought of as an agent, and the trustee can be thought of as a hero. In much of women's political theory, the political agent theory has been prominent. Accordingly, if women best represent women, then they better vote as other women want them to vote.

Based on Skjeie's research on Norwegian women in politics, a third leadership style has emerged. She has identified it as a female style. This style is cooperative, unselfish, communicative, concerned, dialogue- rather than mandate-driven, and emotionally engaged. Women have denied this style as an alternative to the other two. In fact, it may sit between the agent and hero theories of leadership. This communicative theory opposes the idea of politics as a fight. It transforms politics into a forum for consensus building through concrete communication.[44]

The electoral system may be the most important factor in predicting women's leadership percentage. Multiparty political systems and the electoral principle of proportional representation have produced much greater percentages of women leaders than have two-party systems.[45]

As a result of the passage of the Equal Status Act, the role of the Office of the Ombudsperson has become quite important. Without this monitor, the act would not have had the same effect. The act set out to correct an imbalance so it could not be impartial and neutral toward gender until that imbalance was rectified. The act specifies a ban on indirect or de facto discrimination as well as out-right discrimination. The act has opened opportunities for women, and women now have better pay than before the act.[46]

Internationally, there is some precedent for Norway's act. Since 1946, the United Nations (UN) Commission on the Status of Women has worked very hard to improve the position of women around the world. At the First Women's Conference in Mexico in 1975, the member countries decided to create a women's convention, and in 1979 it was adopted by the UN. The Convention on the Elimination of All Forms of Discrimination against Women (CEDAW) wanted to make it clear that human rights applied to women as well. Member states must report to the commission each year.[47]

WOMEN'S ORGANIZATIONS IN SCANDINAVIA

The existence of Nordic women's organizations points to the fact that women have lived in a patriarchal society, and although women have many differences between them, the fact that they are women gives them a common ground for creating such organizations. Women's organizations vary in terms of their membership and focus. Some of these organizations were formed with the expressed purpose of opposing and changing the patriarchal system. The key is that these organizations are communities of women that may differ in their direct purpose but have the same overall goal: the promotion of women's ideas and concerns.[48]

The structure of women's organizations in Scandinavia shows how similar these societies are. In general, there are eight types of women's organizations in Scandinavia:

1. national councils of women's organizations (umbrella organizations)
2. housewives' associations
3. countrywomen's associations
4. the women's movements (woman's rights and feminists)
5. organizations of women in political parties
6. organizations of women in the trade unions
7. social and humanitarian women's agencies
8. religious and temperance societies for women.

Iceland has several trade unions with only women members (i.e., Reykjavik Women's Workers Association). Denmark has a separate trade union for unskilled women workers, Women Worker's Union, with over 90,000 members. The other Nordic countries also had women's trade unions, but they had long since merged into mixed unions. This may be because trade unions in Denmark and Iceland are federations for particular professions (i.e., bricklayers, plumbers, etc.). Unions in Norway, Finland, and Sweden tend to be large industrial unions that encompass an entire industry (e.g., foodstuffs industry).[49]

Women's organizations in Scandinavia, as in other Western societies, can have conflicting interests. Although it could be said that it is in the interest of all women to remove inequality and discrimination and patriarchal oppression, not all women agree on all issues. This stems from the differences in individual women's lives:

1. There are disparities between the situation of the housewife and the woman who works for salary or wage outside the home.
2. There are also inherent economic class divisions among women.
3. There are age differences among women and their perspectives.

The aims and purposes of women's organizations reflect these differences in women's lives. The history of these organizations reveals discord as well as cooperation.[50]

Housewives' associations in Scandinavia represent the viewpoint of equal value for the contributions of men and women. They call for the role of the housewife to be elevated in society as a profession. The Norwegian Women's Public Health Association has also sought similar equal value for their humanitarian and social work that has little real monetary value in a capitalist economy.[51]

The Nordic woman's rights organizations, which formed at the end of the last century, all hold to the ideology of equal status. This ideology is based on the belief that men and women are not as different as the traditional and gender-divided labor market made them out to be. The inherent discrimination of women caused by the differentiation of male and female characteristics needs to be eliminated in order to achieve equal status. Women's demands for equal status in Scandinavia have been supported by the political rise to power of the social democrats and the general ideology of equality propagated by social democracy.[52]

An umbrella organization, the National Council of Women's Organizations, was established in each Nordic country around the turn of the century (except Iceland in 1930). These federations of women's organizations were meant to establish a power base for women in Scandinavia. These councils are organized on the principles of equal value and equal status for women. Their influence has been mainly restricted to issues involving women and children. This was somewhat broadened to include promotion of international arbitration and peace. Their influence has been somewhat limited because of the often conflicting interests of the member groups.[53]

Each political party in the Nordic countries has a women's organization or committee. Parties were always fearful of factionalism and limited many women's groups to youth members, where such groups were useful for recruitment. In 1994, 9 of the 28 party chairpersons in the Nordic countries were women. The

objectives for organizing women within Nordic political parties
have been to persuade women to vote for a particular party, to
recruit women members, to train women for political leadership,
to pursue women's policies both inside and outside the party,
and to encourage cooperation with women in like-minded parties
abroad.[54]

WOMAN'S RIGHTS MOVEMENTS IN SCANDINAVIA

Women's movements were not something new in the 1970s
in Scandinavia. Such associations had been in existence since the
beginning of the twentieth century. The earliest of these Nordic
women's groups was the Danish Women's Society, formed in
1871. The Norwegian Women's Society formed in 1884, the
same year that the Fredrika-Bremer Society in Sweden and the
Suomen Naisyhdistys in Finland were formed. The Icelandic
Women's Rights Association was formed in 1907. Unlike
woman's rights groups in other Western countries, Nordic
groups did not disband after woman suffrage was passed. They
have existed continuously since their inception over 100 years
ago. The 1970s could be characterized as the second high point
in the women's movement in Scandinavia. The first high point
was around the turn of the century.[55]

The second high point of the women's movement in Scandinavia marked a change in the ideological approach of the
woman's rights groups. The new women's movement embraced
an anticapitalist, feminist tinge that highlighted the exploitive
and interwoven nature of patriarchy and capitalism. Women had
been part of socialist movements in the past, of course, but so-
cialism and class distinctions were not part of the woman's rights
groups' agendas. The new women's movement also emphasized
a horizontal organizational structure in keeping with its new emphasis against patriarchy. Smaller groups worked separately for
the whole.[56]

Members of the original women's movement in Scandinavia
were mainly older women, but the new women's movement was

dominated by younger women. These younger women also took on more personal issues (i.e., battering, incest, sex). As in other Western countries, the statement "The personal is political," became the mantra. They also refused to play by the rules of the game, even moving to change gender-specific language, and tended to exclude sympathetic men.[57]

In Denmark, the Redstockings were at the center of the new women's movement. Their organization had a horizontal structure based on consciousness-raising groups, provocative activities, an anticapitalist perspective on women's history, and a break from traditional ideas of the early women's movement. Although the movement gained nationwide attention, it drew its ranks mainly from the middleclass. There were disagreements within the organization in terms of focus of priorities—gender or class struggle.[58]

The Icelandic Redstocking movement began in 1970. By 1974 the organization had established a political agenda connecting class struggle with the women's struggle. Nonsocialist women left the group as a result. As in Denmark, the issue of priorities came into play—whether to focus on class or gender. In spite of this factionalism, women from many different women's organizations in Iceland effectively planned and carried out a women's strike on 24 October 1975. The strike brought the country to a standstill and made headlines around the world. The Redstocking organization eventually splintered but reformed as the Women's Party in 1982. The Icelandic Women's Party had success in the 1983 parliamentary elections.[59]

The New Feminists in Norway based their organization on activities in Denmark and the United States. In 1970 Norwegian women formed consciousness-raising and action groups in Oslo and Bergen. The New Feminists were very similar in ideology to the Redstockings in Denmark—anticapitalist feminism. The Women's Front was formed in 1972 and split away from the New Feminists. The Women's Front held to a more explicit socialist doctrine and a more orthodox organizational structure. Women in the Women's Front struggled with the concept of integration or separation from the male-dominated world. Eventually, the organization was dominated by the Communist Workers' Party, which led to further divisions. The New Feminists, who continued to hold to a more feminist focus, later spun off a Lesbian Movement faction. Divisions within the Norwegian women's liberation movement were more pronounced than in Denmark or Iceland.[60]

Group 8 was formed in Sweden in 1968 with a socialist women's agenda. As in the rest of Scandinavia, most of the members of the new women's liberation movement were from the middleclass. The Women's League in Lund was formed in 1970, followed by more feminist-focused groups later. Group 8 remained the major women's movement organization in Sweden. Group 8 also had ideological struggles with class and gender focus, as in the other Nordic countries. Unlike feminist groups in the rest of Norden, Group 8 retained its early, leaderless, horizontal organizational structure.

The New Women's Liberation Movement did not spread to Finland until 1974. It started first among the Swedish-speaking population. Unionen, the traditional Finnish woman's rights organization, was taken over by younger radicals in 1976. The agenda that had been rather politically neutral up to that point changed to attack the patriarchal society.[61]

FEMININE STYLE OF LEADERSHIP IN SCANDINAVIA?

Despite the high percentage of women in positions of political power in Scandinavia, politics is still a male-dominated arena in Scandinavia and in the rest of the world. Those people who see the direction of change see the increasing numbers of women in politics as positive. Those who look at the relatively slow and isolated growth of women in politics believe that women get elected to political institutions by rules that are dominated by men and such institutions do not draw upon the experiences that are unique to women. Quantitative increases in women leaders do little to change the world for the better, according to those holding such a negative view. Scandinavia's usefulness as a model for other countries may be limited by its uniqueness based on shared cultural values and history. In spite of this fact, certain patterns and experiences in Scandinavia could prove useful for other countries and areas of the world.[62]

Another limitation of women's representation in Scandinavia has been the cabinet posts women have occupied. Women tend to be relegated to positions related to social policy, family and child issues, education, and cultural policy. Men, in contrast, tend to be ministers of finance, industry, justice, defense, and foreign affairs. It should also be noted that Scandinavian women have risen to power relatively fast, mostly in the postwar period, the exception being Finland, where growth has been more gradual. This means that the influence of women is relatively new, and it may take time for women to impact the system they have so recently entered. Bureaucracies tend to take time to change. Disturbing, however, is the slowness by which women are entering corporate positions of leadership in Scandinavia. In this arena Scandinavia ranks no higher than other areas of the Western world.[63]

What difference do numbers make in terms of women in politics? Women have made rapid entrance in politics, but what about other sectors? In Sweden, for example, the Swedish Commission of Inquiry into Democracy and Power found that in 1989, 31 percent of the political leaders were women, 23 percent in the cultural sector, 15 percent in mass media, 5 percent in science and research, and only 1 percent in business sectors. Such statistics indicate that women's entry into politics has not helped them break into leadership positions in other sectors of society. The shrinking institutions theory holds that where women go in, power goes out. In other words, women go into politics, but power is transferred elsewhere. Others point out that the output of the political regimes has little changed since women have come to power. This seems to indicate that Scandinavian politics still reflect largely male values and experiences.[64]

One needs to look at overall societal changes that have occurred during this time that women have broken into politics.
Their progress in politics did not happen in a vacuum. Among
these changes are fundamental demographic changes, the growth
of women's cultural, educational, and economic resources, government policies, and the achievements and influence of the
women's movement.

Scandinavian women have fewer children than before World
War II. They also command almost 50 percent of the labor force
in Scandinavia, most of this growth coming in the 1960s and
1970s. Women's education level is comparable to that of men in
Scandinavia, although women still tend to be overrepresented in
welfare-related fields of study. All of this is closely related to
political changes and the subsequent equality legislation in all
Scandinavian countries. The trends are manifested and guaran-
teed by legislative action. One cannot discount the central role of
Scandinavian governments in establishing woman's rights. There
has been a steady flow of favorable reforms for women in Scandinavia in the postwar period. Women have been empowered
through their increased participation in grassroots political organizations. The remarkable fact is that all of this happened
rather quickly. Gender differences in politics evaporated as more
women took center stage.[65]

In Norway, women politicians stand out because of their
softer attitudes and feminine experiences, according to Arne
Strand, former state secretary for Prime Minister Brundtland.
Brundtland, as an example, could show great emotion and even
cry in public. This is true of other Norwegian women politicians
as well. Men are required to control their emotions more than
women are. Women politicians in Norway have different political priorities than men. They are interested more in social issues—especially children's issues and health reform. Strand
noted that without so many women politicians, Norway probably
would not have as many child-care centers. Beyond the easier
display of emotion and different interests in politics, Strand did
not notice any other significant differences between male and
female politicians in Norway. He stressed that women are just as

skilled as politicians, just as tough and ambitious, and just as astute on economic issues and show no differences from men in conducting foreign policy. Contrary to what many people believe, Strand continued, the environmental movement in Norway was not dominated by women. In fact, the first environmental minister was a man. "Fifteen years ago it was a problem to be a woman in politics," according to Strand. "This was especially true in the trade unions. Now, gender is less of a problem."[66]

What is it about Norwegian society that allows for more women in political leadership positions? Strand holds that Norwegians have sought equality at all levels, school, universities, and the workplace. It is now just as likely for a man to be at home with the kids as a woman. Family leave is required for both men and women. Women are more politically active than men at the grassroots level and in the universities. According to Strand, it is an advantage to be a woman today in Norway. Top-level politics in Norway is now dominated by women. It all began in the Labor Party and with Gro Harlem Brundtland. She was there at the right time with the right skills.[67]

Strand concluded that women politicians do not have the same support network as men, so they have to work harder. Without the quota system, the political landscape would not have changed so fast. When asked if he believed that more social justice is created with women political leaders, Strand disagreed. "Look at Thatcher," he said; "political currents go deeper than just whether or not a leader is a man or a woman." Strand added that political discussions often went better when there were a man and a woman involved, instead of two women.[68]

In an interview, Henrik Width, the political editor of the *Aftenposten* in Oslo, agreed with Arne Strand that women leaders tend to show their feelings more, that they are more sensitive, and that they cry more often. This does not happen with men, according to Width, and women can get away with it. He was quick to point out that you cannot talk about women in Norwegian politics without talking about Brundtland. She was at the leading edge of the change, and her influence in Norway is pervasive. Since Brundtland came to power, a woman has at one time or another been in charge of all major political parties in Norway. Width noted that Brundtland was a remarkable leader and would be considered strong whether she was a man or a woman. She listened well and was not easily shaken by political turmoil. The decision to institute a quota system was criticized by some, but almost everyone agreed that something had to be done to get more women into political office. Width agreed with Strand that women leaders tend to pay more attention to social welfare issues and policies related to children and education. Unlike Strand, Width noted that the main objective for either male or female politicians in Norway has been maintaining a sound economy that can provide for the social welfare.[69]

An interesting phenomenon in Norwegian politics is that the political center of the system has moved slightly to the right. The Labor Party has become more conservative. In the 1970s the Labor Party had more socialist dogma. Width said that Brundtland and the Labor Party "stole the conservative party's clothes." They take popular conservative causes and make them their own. Width added that the political system in Norway is easier to change because of its small size, which makes it relatively easy to regulate. He saw no credence in the power shift or shrinking institutions thesis, which holds that power now rests in the private sector, and that is why women are in the public sector. As evidence against that theory, he noted that government spending has increased with more women in government. Width said that there are fewer women in private sector leadership because there are no encouragement for them and no debate, different methods are needed to get in, and there is less turnover in corporate management.[70]

Henrik Width saw no difference in the decision-making abilities of men and women. He believed that differences lay more along party lines than along gender. Brundtland was a very skilled politician and good at finding the middle path. There is a growing sense in Norway that men must work with women, and there is no sense of female revenge against men in the political system. Norway has a tolerant system of politics, Width noted; everything is not black and white, right or wrong. There is a need to cooperate with other parties, kind of a balancing act. This contributes to the idea that the society is equal.[71]

Gender in political leadership, according to Width, does not really matter. Reforms since the 1980s emerged from the whole of Norwegian society realizing that change was needed. He believes that this was not just owing to women in power. Width also believes that the decision against membership in the European Union in a 1995 vote was affected not so much by women as by the conflict between urban and rural Norway.[72]

In an interview with Hanne Skartveit, the political editor from *Verdens Gang* or *VG*, she pointed out that women leaders in Norway tend to focus more on details, are better prepared, and cannot afford to make as many mistakes as the male leaders. In contrast to Strand, Skartveit noted that women politicians have formed a women's network, like the old boys' network. However, she said, women tend to be harder on each other than on men. She felt that women politicians tend to be more cooperative, more careful, and, agreeing with Strand and Width, more emotional. She noted, as did Strand and Width, that the controversial quota system has contributed to the great number of women leaders in Norway.[73]

Skartveit said that there had been a tradition of strong women in Norway, maybe because of the way industrialization came to Norway. The Industrial Revolution was slow in reaching Norway, and once it did arrive, it developed slowly. This slow evolution of industrialization minimized the impact on the family and on the importance of women's roles. Skartveit also said that women's organizations in Norway are very strong. She agreed with Strand and Width that women leaders focus on child-care and parental leave policies. She did not note any differences between male and female politicians in terms of economic or defense policy making. She concluded that feminine leadership differs in more subtle ways and, agreeing with Strand, that most differences are due to party affiliation rather than gender. Men do seem willing to take more risks, she added, and women will take on stronger roles in economics and defense when they gain more experience.[74]

In an interview with Grete Berget, then Norwegian minister for family and children, Berget said she had been in the Labor Party for twenty years prior to being named to her cabinet post. She came from a working-class background, where the most important thing for her growing up was that there should not be differences between men and women in terms of ability. She was a leader in party organizations as a child and always thought that women could do the same job as men. The belief was that women should share power, not take over and push others out to advance. Women have different experiences than men, and women tend to have more to do with everyday family life. She noted that since women have come to power, Norway has the best maternity leave policy in Europe. Norway has doubled the number of kindergartens since the 1986 women's government. Berget believes that women round the sharp corners in politics and are better listeners and organizers than men. Men could never, in the past, miss a meeting because of child-care problems. Now, because women have entered leadership positions and have missed meetings to care for their children, men can also miss meetings. Berget, as a cabinet minister, was gone for three months with her new baby.[75]

Women's style of political leadership can vary, according to Berget. Even though women do not all have the same style of leadership, Berget noted that women do tend to be clearer in what they mean and, contrary to Skartveit, that they do not have a women's version of the old boys' support network. Women tend to check everything and are more careful than men. Women are individualistic in getting their work done—they do not delegate as much as men. They rely on themselves and take longer to make a decision. Women are not good at supporting each other because of this tendency. Women tend to slow down the process of decision making and are not quick to support an issue. Berget also felt that women politicians are more sensitive to criticism, especially from the media, which are still male-dominated in Norway.[76]

According to Berget, Norway has changed remarkably in recent history. Twenty years ago, only 20 percent of married women worked; now 80 percent do. Norwegian society is better off now that it has mixed the experiences of men and women. Women have become a powerful force in politics in Norway. When asked if she thought that women in government would create more social justice and peace, Berget responded; "Women would tend to discuss more, are less likely to jump in with military solutions . . . women have a non-military tradition, so they are therefore less likely to use the military."[77]

Norwegian political researcher Hege Skeije feels that women's integration into politics was based on stereotypes. However, she notes, stereotypes in Norway are not as strong as in America. People may perceive a female leadership style, but the picture is hard to maintain because there are so many different women and styles. Stereotypes that concern form are more dangerous than those that concern content. As an example, Skeije noted Norwegian newspaper coverage of the first women's cabinet in 1986-89. They called the women cabinet ministers "little men in dresses: Do we really need women if they look just like men?" These women cabinet ministers tended to pronounce male ideals. In spite of this, Skeije felt that it was important to get women into the political structure because policy content for women was more important than style. As an example, Skeije mentioned that Prime Minister Brundtland used different ways of achieving her goals. She could be a gender-neutral boss, but her enemies said she was more administrator than politician. She eventually became the mother of the nation. One of her most valuable assets as a politician was that she could change with the times.[78]

In the mid-1970s most political women were members of women's organizations. There was a collective effort to get women into politics and to appeal to women voters. Access was the key to success. Traditional party politics in Norway tended to be too hierarchical, yet politics in all of Scandinavia is less strident than in the United States. The emphasis was still on social democracy. The Labor Party's dedication to social democracy was a good foundation for aspiring women politicians.

According to Skeije, the early feminist political agenda was limited—ideas tied to economic independence and motherhood and gender relations. There has been incremental movement to ward gender balance in Norway tied to women's coming to positions of political leadership. Asked if it would be a more peaceful world with women politicians, Skeije said that women in Norway have tended to be against many defense projects. An example was women's opposition to the prepositioning of strategic nuclear missiles by the North Atlantic Treaty Organization (NATO) in Norway. Skeije's main criticism of the most prominent Norwegian woman politician, Prime Minister Brundtland, was that she had moved the Labor Party to the right politically, with the exception of policies dealing with women's issues and the environment.[79]

In order to understand more deeply the role of women leaders in society, the next chapter analyzes, in detail, the political ascendancy and administration of three female national leaders—former Norwegian prime minister Gro Harlem Brundtland, former Icelandic president Vigdis Finnbogadottir, and former president Violetta Chamorro of Nicaragua (to provide an international point of comparison).

NOTES

1. Technically, the term "Norden" refers to all five Nordic countries: Norway, Iceland, Sweden, Denmark, and Finland. Scandinavia usually refers only to Norway, Sweden, and Denmark. For the purposes of this book, I use the more common term "Scandinavia" to mean all five Nordic countries.

2. Infant mortality rates vary from 5 to 6 per 1,000 live births for girls, 5 to 8 per 1,000 live births for boys. The average life expectancy at birth ranges from 78 to 81 for women, and from 72 to 76 for men. In 1992 fertility rates varied from 1.8 to 2.2 children per woman.

3. Elina Haavio-Mannila and Torild Skard, "The Arena for Political Activity: The Position of Women in Nordic Societies Today," in Elina Haavio-Mannila, Drude Dahlerup, Maud Eduards, Esther Gudmundsdóttir, Beatrice Halsaa, Helga Maria Hernes, Eva Hänninen-

Salmelin, Bergthora Sigmundsdóttir, Sirkka Sinkkonen, and Torild Skard, eds., *Unfinished Democracy: Women in Nordic Politics* (New York: Pergamon Press, 1985), pp. 1-2; Nordic Council of Ministers, *Women and Men in the Nordic Countries: Facts and Figures 1994* (Copenhagen, Denmark: Nord 1994:3), p. 10.

4. Nordic Council of Ministers, p. 10.

5. Haavio-Mannila and Skard, p. 2.

6. Nordic Council of Ministers, p. 11.

7. Nordic Council of Ministers, p. 11.

8. Jill M. Bystydzienski, ed., *Women Transforming Politics: Worldwide Strategies for Empowerment* (Bloomington: Indiana University Press, 1992), pp. 205-6.

9. Norway has 36 percent, Sweden 34 percent, Finland 32 percent, Denmark 31 percent, and Iceland 22 percent.

10. Hege Skjeie, "The Rhetoric of Difference: On Women's Inclusion into Political Elites," *Politics and Society* 19, no. 2 (June 1991), 235.

11. Mim Kelber, ed., *Women and Government: New Ways to Political Power* (Westport, CT: Praeger, 1994), 61-62; Marit Tovsen, "Women in Politics in Norway." Seminar paper for Women from Eastern Europe, Denmark, 19 August 1992, mimeograph, p. 3; Erna Solberg, Member of Parliament, Bergen, Norway. Interviews conducted 8-10 March 1995 in Seattle, Washington.

12. Norwegian Equal Status Council, "Women in Politics: Equality and Empowerment." 1994, Oslo, Norway, pp. 1-9.

13. Tovsen, 4; Solberg interview.

14. Bruce O. Solheim, *The Nordic Nexus: A Lesson in Peaceful Security* (Westport, CT: Praeger, 1994), p. 38.

15. However, the social democrats have often been divided on issues. Solberg interview; Solheim, pp. 24-26.

16. Barbara G. Haskel, *The Scandinavian Option:Opportunities and Opportunity Costs in Postwar Scandinavian Foreign Policies* (Oslo, Norway: Universitetsforlaget, 1976), pp. 14-15.

17. Haskel, pp. 16-17.

18. From this type of political culture, the Social Democratic Party evolved. In 1920 the average percentage of social democratic vote in Scandinavia was 31 percent. By 1929 all of the Social Democratic Parties in the Nordic region were firmly established, except in Iceland. By the 1950s the percentage of the social democratic vote had risen to over 40 percent. Francis G. Castles, *The Social Democratic Image of Soci-*

ety: A Study of the Achievements and Origins of Scandinavian Social Democracy in Comparative Perspective (Boston: Routledge & Kegan Paul, 1978), p. 6.

19. Steven Kelman, *Regulating America, Regulating Sweden* (Cambridge, MA: MIT Press, 1981), pp. 119-20, 232-33.

20. Three aspects of the development of Nordic labor movements were influential in determining their strength, unity, and integration:

1. the relative absence of impediments to working-class industrial and political organization,
2. the timing and social context of organizational growth, and
3. the nature of the strategic choices made by the movements.

The response by authorities in the Nordic region to labor organization and protest was quite mild in comparison to the rest of Europe. Although there was substantial unrest—1848-51 in Norway, 1871-77 in Denmark, and 1876 in Sweden—by the 1890s freedom of industrial and political organization was the general rule throughout Scandinavia. Kelman, pp. 13-14.

21. Kelman, pp. 22-38.

22. This is a pattern that should be applicable to other regions as well.

23. Francis G. Castles, "Scandinavia: The Politics of Stability," in Roy C. Macridis, ed., *Modern Political Systems: Europe*, 5th ed. (Englewood Cliffs, NJ: Prentice-Hall, 1983), pp. 421-22; Solheim, pp. 41-43; and Peter J. Katzenstein, *Small States in World Markets: Industrial Policy in Europe* (Ithaca, NY: Cornell University Press, 1985), pp. 97, 101.

24. Nordic Council of Ministers, p. 11.

25. Nordic Council of Ministers, pp. 12-13.

26. Nordic Council of Ministers, p. 17.

27. Tovsen, pp. 4-5.

28. Kelber, pp. 62-63, 65, 66-68; Tovsen, 6; Solberg interview; Nordic Council of Ministers, pp. 34-36; Norwegian Royal Ministry of Children and Family Affairs, "Gender Equality in Norway." The National Report to the Fourth UN Conference on Women in Beijing, 1995, Oslo, Norway, pp. 8-18.

29. Kelber, pp. 70-72; Tovsen, pp. 7-11; Solberg interview; Norwegian Equal Status Ombud, "The Norwegian Equal Status Act with Comments," 1989, Oslo, Norway.

30. Norwegian Equal Status Act Ombud, p. 4.

31. Kelber, p. 76.

32. Kelber, p. 80.

33. The structurally conditioned and veiled aspects of the oppression of women today may be illustrated by what I call women's integration into superfluous or shrinking institutions. Women, as it were, inherit from men positions that have become insignificant or less important as departure points for power and influence. Hege Skjeie, "The Feminization of Power: Norway's Political Experiment (1986-)," Oslo: Institut for Samfunsforskning Rapport 88:8, August 1988, p. 4.

34. Hege Skjeie, "The Uneven Advance of Norwegian Women," *New Left Review* 187 (May/June 1991), 82.

35. Skjeie, "Uneven Advance," p. 84.

36. Skjeie, "Uneven Advance," p. 86.

37. Skjeie, "Uneven Advance," p. 87.

38. Skjeie, "Uneven Advance," p. 90.

39. Skjeie, "Uneven Advance," p. 93.

40. Skjeie, "Uneven Advance," p. 93.

41. Skjeie, "Uneven Advance," p. 94.

42. Skjeie, "Uneven Advance," p. 101.

43. Hege Skjeie, "Politisk Lederskap," *Nytt Norsk Tidsskrift* (2/1992), pp. 122-23.

44. Skjeie, "Politisk Lederskap," p. 120.

45. Skjeie, "The Feminization of Power," p. 2.

46. Sigrun Hoel, "Moving Towards Real Rights for Women—The Legal Strategy" (Oslo, Norway: Norwegian Labor Party, 1994), mimeograph, pp. 7-9.

47. Hoel, p. 12.

48. Haavio-Mannila and Skard, pp. 6-7.

49. Haavio-Mannila and Skard, pp. 8-9. See also: Anna Caspari Agerholt, *Den Norske Kvinnebevegelses Historie* (Oslo, Norway: 1937); Gyrithe Lemche, *Dansk Kvindesamfunds Historie gennem 40 ar* (Copenhagen, Denmark: 1939); Marta von Alftan, *Sietseman vuosikymata Naisasialiitto Unionin Historia* (publishing information unknown); Lydia Wahlstrom, *Den Svenska Kvinnororelsen* (Stockholm, Sweden: 1933); *Kvenrettindafelag Islands ara 1907-1947* (Rejkjavik, Iceland: 1947).

50. Drude Dahlerup and Brita Gulli, "Women's Organizations in the Nordic Countries," in Haavio-Mannila and Skard, pp. 10-11.

51. Dahlerup and Gulli, p. 11.

52. Dahlerup and Gulli, pp. 12-13.

53. Dahlerup and Gulli, pp. 14-15.

54. Dahlerup and Gulli, pp. 16-17; Nordic Council of Ministers, p. 35.

55. Dahlerup and Gulli, pp. 22-23.

56. Dahlerup and Gulli, pp. 24-25.

57. Dahlerup and Gulli, pp. 25-26.

58. Dahlerup and Gulli, pp. 26-27.

59. Dahlerup and Gulli, pp. 27-28.

60. Dahlerup and Gulli, p. 28.

61. Dahlerup and Gulli, pp. 29-30.

62. Lauri Karvonen and Per Selle, eds., *Women in Nordic Politics: Closing the Gap* (Brookfield, VT: Dartmouth, 1995), pp. 4-5.

63. Karvonen and Selle, pp. 5-6.

64. Karvonen and Selle, pp. 7-8.

65. Karvonen and Selle, pp. 8-9.

66. Arne Strand, Deputy Chief Editor, *Arbeiderbladet,* Oslo, Norway, and former State Secretary for Prime Minister Gro Harlem Brundtland, 1987-1989. Interview, conducted on 3 July 1995 in Oslo.

67. Strand interview.

68. Strand interview.

69. Henrik Width, Political Editor, *Aftenposten*, Oslo, Norway. Interview, conducted 27 June 1995 in Oslo.

70. Width interview.

71. Width interview.

72. Width interview.

73. Hanne Skartveit, Political Editor, *Verdens Gang (VG)*, Oslo, Norway. Interview, conducted 29 June 1995 in Oslo.

74. Skartveit interview.

75. Grete Berget, State Cabinet Minister for Family and Children, Oslo, Norway. Interview, conducted 30 June 1995.

76. Berget interview.

77. Berget interview.

78. Hege Skeije, Researcher, Institutt for Samfunnsforskning, Oslo, Norway. Interview, conducted 28 June 1995 in Oslo, Norway.

79. Skeije interview.

Chapter 3

Profiles of Three Women Political Leaders

> If you speak with authority, mean what you say, say
> it strongly, clearly ... then people will listen, whether
> you are a man or a woman.
> —Gro Harlem Brundtland

> Women's leadership should not be viewed as exclu-
> sionary, but as an integral component leading toward
> a society in which a question of male and female
> leadership has become irrelevant.
> —Vigdis Finnbogadottir

> I am not a feminist . . . I am a woman dedicated to
> my home.
> —Violetta Chamorro

This chapter closely examines the ascendancy of three different
women leaders. Two are from Scandinavia, owing to the main
focus of this book, and one is from the developing world. Because Scandinavian society is quite unique and has often been
carelessly used as a model for other societies to emulate, this
comparison of women leaders also examines a non-Scandinavian
leader.

GRO HARLEM BRUNDTLAND

In a "quiet corner" of Europe has grown a movement toward gender equality in government. The Nordic region (Norden) leads the world in terms of percentage of women in national legislatures or parliaments. Two of the five Nordic countries, Norway and Iceland, have recently had women as their national chief executives.[1] This remarkable achievement can be attributed to the political culture in Scandinavia. Norwegian prime minister Gro Harlem Brundtland has done much to change the place of women in Norwegian and Nordic political life and stands to change the place of women worldwide as well. As U.S. feminist leader Gloria Steinem writes:

After decades of answering questions about Golda Meier, Indira Gandhi, Margaret Thatcher, and other imitative but pioneering examples of women leaders who proved that women could do "a man's job," activists in women's movements around the world now have Prime Minister Gro Harlem Brundtland of Norway, a feminist pioneer at the top. As the first elected world leader to come to power on the issues of, and supported by, this modern wave of feminism, she is much less imitative of what has gone before.[2]

Nordic countries have the highest levels of female representation in the world because of their political cultures and electoral systems. Nordic societies are based on egalitarianism with a heavy emphasis on social justice. Critics note that although women have made advancements in the public sector, they still fall behind in the private sector, where men still dominate.[3] However, in the political sphere, the Nordic societies have no peers when it comes to gender equality. The second reason for Scandinavia's achievement is tied to the electoral systems. The proportional representation system in Scandinavia generates a greater number of parties than does a single-member-district-plurality or "winner-take-all" electoral system. Many of these parties advocate woman's rights. Several representatives can be chosen in some districts so that women can gain representation without taking on entrenched powers within more established parties. Also, party lists are used instead of individual candidates. These lists emerge from district nominating conventions, where the situation is ideal for highly motivated advocates for equitable representation.[4]

With the exception of Einar Gerhardsen, Brundtland sat in power the longest as prime minister of Norway and has been one of the strongest political figures in Norwegian history. She has also established an international reputation. She was an accomplished politician who promoted the role of women in power and established herself as an international environmental leader. Her influence within the Norwegian Labor Party led to the party's supporting Norwegian membership in the European Community (EC)—a reversal from an earlier party position. She has been in the forefront of Norwegian politics since the 1970s.[5]

Gro was born on 20 April 1939 into a comfortable situation. One of four children, Gro lived with her grandmother in Sweden during part of the German occupation of Norway in World War II. After the war, her family was intimate with the family of Prime Minister Einar Gerhardsen. Brundtland was familiar with the Labor Party inner circle early on.[6]

In some ways, her career seemed to parallel her father's. He was a doctor, which Gro later became as well, until Gerhardsen asked him to be social minister in 1955. Later he moved to the Defense Department. But her father was not the only active political figure in her life; Gro's grandmother was active as a secretary at the Labor Party headquarters for over 30 years.[7]

Gro Harlem Brundtland went to medical school at Harvard in 1960. After finishing her medical degree, she served as the assistant medical director of the Oslo Board of Health. In the 1970s she made a name for herself in politics when she took on the Conservative Party over its press campaign to ban abortion.[8] She felt that it was her "obligation as a professional, and as a woman and a politically concerned person, to start writing in the press." After this media exposure, she was then asked to enter the cabinet. It was quite clear the prime minister was looking for a woman to replace the previous female minister of health and social affairs, who had died.[9] Many people noted her lack of political experience, but Brundtland did not let this criticism go unanswered. She said that

there is a very close connection between being a physician and being a politician. The doctor first tries to prevent illness, then tries to treat it if it comes. It is exactly the same as what you try to do as a politician, but with regard to society.[10]

On 29 August 1974 Norwegian prime minster Trygve Bratteli summoned the 35-year-old Gro Harlem Brundtland to his office in Oslo. He offered her the position of environment minister. She had not been previously elected to any public national office, and her only experience had been in student government and working for the Norwegian Labor Party. This opened the door for her rise to the top.[11]

Brundtland was energetic and was accused of stepping on some toes and for moving too fast on some issues. She was known to show great emotion in debate. On one occasion, she became so intense during a speech that she broke a ballpoint pen in pieces on the podium.[12] Brundtland also angered some industrialists in her position as minister of the environment. She helped establish nature preserves and pleaded for preservation and protection of the natural beauty of Norway threatened by offshore oil drilling.[13]

Brundtland and two others represented the only three women in the Labor government in 1974. She was labeled a new feminist, but she was not really the standard-bearer for women in the 1970s. She never belonged to the Labor Party's women's movement, nor had she been a member of any feminist group. She admitted to feeling spoiled in some ways because her domestic situation was so stable, but she soon learned that, in government, men and women had different concerns. Her contact with middle-class and lower-middle-class women, once she had entered the government, led her to gain a new and valuable social perspective.[14]

In April 1975 she became head of the Norwegian Labor Party. She was the first woman in Norwegian history to hold that position. Detractors have pointed out that the main reason she became head of the party was that she was a woman, and 1975 was the international year of the woman. In reality, the party probably saw that she was politically powerful and could get things done.[15]

Brundtland was not satisfied with status quo politics in Norway. She reflected a new style. She possessed a great intellect, she was quick to learn in the world of male politics, she had a strong political ambition, and she was willing to take brave stands on issues she held as vital to the country (i.e., the EC vote in 1972, where she went against the party leadership's stand). From the 1972 EC mobilization and politicization of Norway emerged two movements, the feminist and the environmental movements. Academics were also making headway into the party apparatus. With Gro's emergence on the political scene, all three of these movements seemed to have one head.[16]

As environment minister, Gro received a lot of attention from a tragedy in 1977. A fire at an oil platform named Ekofisk in the North Sea shocked the nation. Norwegians wondered how such a thing could happen with all the new technology and precautions. The spill cost the country a great deal of money, and, as a result, offshore drilling was indefinitely postponed. She handled the situation very effectively in an emotionally charged atmosphere. An American reporter said that her intelligence and charm were such that "no one could bring out the knives." She took charge, answered difficult questions, and came out of the whole affair as a popular and well-known environmentalist.[17]

Brundtland took a little-known Ministry of the Environment and elevated it into the political mainstream during her five years as its head. However, a power shift in the Labor Party in the late 1970s shifted the party's focus from growth to defense. Her presence in the party and in Norwegian politics was growing, so it was natural for her to assume that she would be put into a more important ministry. But then the Labor Party was set back in the late 1970s. The Conservative Party came into power. Norwegians were suffering through tough economic times, and many young voters seemed to lack direction. The political climate seemed to call for less regulation and more freedom. Subsequently, since the Labor Party seemed to represent the opposite of where the political mainstream was heading, its leadership floundered.[18]

Brundtland ran for Parliament in 1977 and won, but her seat had to be held by a proxy as she was still in the cabinet. In 1979 she resigned from the cabinet and took her seat in the Storting (the Norwegian Parliament). Ostensibly, this was to gain experience to groom her for the prime minister role.[19]

Gro Harlem Brundtland may have been the only prime minister to come to power because of a misunderstanding. Only one of the six Labor Party leaders who met in February 1981 favored her for the position of prime minister—Gro herself. It had been prearranged that Rolf Hansen would take over for Prime Minister Odvar Nordli, but at the meeting Hansen turned down the invitation, causing Nordli to become rattled and upset. Apparently, Nordli had misunderstood Hansen, who said that he would think about the offer but not that he would definitely accept it. Hansen had subsequently come to see the advantage of supporting Brundtland. But Nordli did not know this, and Brundtland emerged as the prime minister. When the press met them after the meeting, Gro could hardly keep the joy from her face. Brundtland does not agree with this account. She says that the party wanted a woman as prime minister, but the leadership wanted her to step forward herself and not have it appear that she was pushed.

She succeeded Odvar Nordli, who was retiring ostensibly for reasons of health. Other factors included the slow and steady decline of the Labor Party in opinion polls and dissension within the party. She was chosen partly to dampen the strength of the Right in Norwegian politics. The Labor Party had been slipping since the EC vote in 1973. There was an understandable desire to replace a weary man with an energetic person who could better unite the party, bridge the difference, and, hopefully, ensure more popular support before the September elections. Gro got not only Rolf Hansen's support but also, by way of her father, Einar Gerhardsen's. That, combined with her grassroots appeal and will to power, brought her into the prime minister's office in 1981. Norway got its first woman prime minister (she was the first in Scandinavia as well).[20]

Brundtland's path to power was short. It took her six years in state politics before she became prime minister. And she was prime minister for only two months before the Labor Party made her their leader as well. She had both ambition and the will to power. There were those in the party who thought her rise to the top was too fast. But the grass roots of the party wanted her. She knew of the criticism, but she made up for her lack of experience with an incredible work ethic and energy for the job.[21]

Brundtland was the first Norwegian prime minister to go by a first name. Many feminists thought that this was a form of discrimination, since she was a woman, and no male prime minster had been called by his first name. She said that if it is discrimination, it is good discrimination, and she did not mind. The papers spoke of "Gro-Time," and the "Gro-Wave."[22] Some critics pointed out that Brundtland was brought to power only due to economic troubles in Norway and a growing sense of cynicism. She admitted that sometimes the atmosphere seemed to indicate that she and the other women ministers she had brought in were expected "to do the dishes after the party."[23]

After taking over, the Labor Party government announced a price freeze and issued a warning to conservatives to stop trying to dismantle the welfare state. Despite this, Labor lost the elections in October 1981, and conservative Kåre Willoch moved into the prime minster's office, ousting Brundtland, but Brundtland did not slow down. She accepted an invitation to work on Swedish prime minister Olaf Palme's Independent Commission on Disarmament and Security. She also worked on the United Nations World Commission on Environment and Development with members from 22 countries. Hers was a strong voice for environmentalism: "There is an urgent need to fashion a long-term, integrated global strategy for survival on this planet. We need a strategy for common survival and common security, a strategy for a common future." In 1983, UN general secretary Javier Pérez de Cuellar asked her to chair the commission.[24]

Brundtland became prime minister again in 1986, when the conservatives lost power. This time the Labor Party had been working on gender equality within its ranks. Under Brundtland's second government, the Labor Party shifted more toward the center; some said, to the right. Compromise was needed to stay in power. Brundtland built a cabinet that included seven women. She said that a "natural balance of men and women makes preju-diced decisions less likely and gives the greatest possible breadth of experience." Furthermore, her example could influence other countries as well, according to Brita Westergaard of Norway's Equal Status Council. The cabinet addressed broader issues once in power. These included an expansion of day care and an exten-sion of paid maternity leave from 18 to 26 weeks. Since 1981 the Labor Party required that 40 percent of its candidates for public office be women.[25]

Because Brundtland appointed a cabinet in which nearly half the ministers were women, an international media sensation emerged. The *Wall Street Journal* dedicated its front page to the story: "A Distressed Norway Counts on Its Women to Set Things Right." Brundtland was chosen as woman of the year in *Ms.* magazine. By 1991 half of the major political parties in Norway had chosen women as leaders. Norway's percentage of women in Parliament grew to more than 36 percent, compared to below 10 percent in the early 1970s. Yet, in the private sector, little changed in terms of women's sharing positions of leadership.[26]

Brundtland faced great economic problems in her second term. Norway's oil revenues were dropping, and inflation was high. By 1985 Norway's offshore oil drilling accounted for 20 percent of its gross national product (GNP). Being a small coun-try with few other economic assets and an expensive state wel-fare system, Norway was becoming increasingly dependent on oil revenue. She put a cap on wages, devalued the Norwegian krone, and cut down on consumer credits. Her foreign policy was based on NATO membership, but she did not hesitate to criticize U.S. president Ronald Reagan's policies in Nicaragua or his Strategic Defense Initiative. She also had Washington cooling its heels in 1986, when she banned American F-111 fighter-bombers from Norwegian airspace during allied military exercises. Brundtland's policies were in keeping with the social democratic tradition in Scandinavia of avoiding big power confrontation through balancing security interests. In her words: "Norwegian territory must not be seen to be a threat to its neighbors."[27]

Norway had great sympathy for the Third World and maintained one of the world's highest foreign-aid-to-GNP ratios. Her leadership on the UN World Commission on Environment and Development became well known with the publication of the *Brundtland Report* in 1987. In this report she noted that

We must think globally and in a long-term perspective. No single region or nation can isolate itself from the rest of the world ... the global environment cannot be separated from political, economic, and moral issues. Environmental concerns must permeate all decisions, from consumer choices through national budgets to international agreements. We must learn to accept the fact that environmental considerations are part of the unified management of our planet.[28]

In spite of her international environmental leadership, she has been criticized by environmental groups, especially in Norway. To this she says: "I don't know of any environmental group that does not view its government as an adversary."[29] Brundtland explained her view on the economy and the environment in 1987:

The industrialized world has taken energy for granted, in the 1970s it became an issue and crisis. Energy was a major part of Our Common Future from the UN Commission. We can solve energy and social problems through economic growth. Ecology and economies can grow together in a growing process. Then relations between and in nations will stabilize.[30]

An incident that occurred during a campaign trip in 1989 tells much about Brundtland. On a campaign plane trip in bad weather one of the members of the press collapsed on board. At first everyone panicked until someone remembered that Gro was a doctor as well as a politician. She dropped her paperwork and attended the ailing man. When another photographer tried to capture the moment on film, Brundtland would not allow it. She made it clear that this was not a photo opportunity.[31]

In September 1989 she was voted out of office again, in spite of her rising international popularity. She remained out only until November 1990, when she came up with a new compromise with the oil producers and a favorable position on EC membership for Norway. There was even talk late in 1991 that Brundtland would succeed Cuellar as UN secretary-general. Although she did not get the UN position, she did play a prominent role at the Earth Summit in Rio de Janeiro in June 1992, where she said:

A sharp reduction in the arms race and the expected peace dividend can be used to finance today's most urgent form of collective security— environmental security. We should not be surprised that developing nations are approaching the Rio summit with open economic demands. For them, it is essentially a conference about development and justice ... sustainable development can be advanced only by an international trading system which enlarges freedom of market access, especially for developing countries and which incorporates environmental values.[32]

Although she is often viewed as a feminist leader, Brundtland defines her leadership as multidimensional. "Women's roles and their chances in life to develop themselves are central to my thinking, but I am not a one-issue person." She says that feminism does not mean you should not fulfill your biological and psychological role as a mother; "then I think it's far off track." Brundtland holds that feminism is the promotion of real female interest, including a woman's being able to bear children if she wants. According to Brundtland: "It is not only a question of bringing women into the old roles of men, but also of bringing men into the old roles of women. I believe that a better society will be created from this."[33] Brundtland carries with her a strong sense of social responsibility that transfers to the foreign policy of Norway. "If you are born strong, you have an even stronger responsibility for the people who didn't get the same start."[34]

Frequently, her political opponents have made fun of Brundtland's politically conservative husband, political scientist

Arne Olav Brundtland. During one point, the conservatives had a slogan: "Do as Gro does: Choose a conservative." But she countered with the slogan: "Do as Arne does, choose Gro." When asked if their political differences affect their marriage, Gro replied: "Does anyone ever ask a man in politics how he can live with a spouse who doesn't espouse his views?"[35]

As Brundtland rose through the political ranks, there were reactions from her male counterparts. She met with hostility, but much of it was orchestrated by the opposition party. She admitted that it was difficult to be the first woman prime minister of Norway. Brundtland liked to tell the story of a news correspondent's child who was watching television just after she had been ousted from the prime minister's office. The child asked her father, "Daddy, on television today they said that a man was Prime Minister. Is it possible that a man can be Prime Minister?"[36]

Brundtland's government in 1986 considered not only gender but also political experience. Although the Labor Party is not sure what women will do to change politics, it is dedicated to putting women in leadership positions. Research has shown that the women politicians in Norway have been very concerned with issues related to wages, maternity leave, day care, and other social care reforms. One might note that men have also championed these reforms, but that is not news. Although many of the women politicians supported these caring issues, those who were members of the women's movement went their own way once in office. In spite of this indication of supporting these caring issues, Norwegian feminist researcher Hege Skjeie could find no clear women's political power mandate.[37]

Hege Skjeie interviewed one of Brundtland's cabinet ministers, who said that personal power determined results in politics. She gave the example of how she worked for child-care reforms for years in lower levels of government to no avail. But once she had been appointed to a cabinet level, her personal power enabled her to make the changes she had been working so long to attain. The Brundtland government tended to emphasize those things that united, rather than divided, in relation to gender. This has precluded any serious male backlash. The lesson in Norwegian politics is that women must develop themselves not as a woman stereotype but as leaders themselves. The balance of interest becomes critical. Gender conflict has been avoided because of the tendency to seek compromise and consensus instead of charging ahead with vitriolic rhetoric. Maybe women have entered politics in Norway based on gender, but they have proven themselves to be effective leaders. This has been in spite of comments in the press that have been ill conceived. In one such incident a Norwegian newspaper called Brundtland's cabinet "good little men in dresses."[38]

According to Arne Strand, former state secretary to Prime Minister Brundtland, her strong points were her work ethic, experience, intelligence, ability to get people to work together, and abilities as an administrator and that she is a woman. Negative points for Brundtland were that she had too little ideological orientation, and she was pragmatic at all times. She never really had good relations with the trade unions, and she often had trouble with her temper. She also had trouble speaking sometimes, in that she was not always very precise. Remarkably, 96 percent of the Norwegian people thought she did a great job. She showed resilience; she kept going after the defeat of EC membership for Norway, which she supported. She was not afraid to tell reporters that they were dumb or that they asked stupid questions. She also was known not to know when a joke was funny. Brundtland often asked Strand to tell her when a joke was funny.[39]

According to Henrik Width, the political editor of the *Aftenposten*, he was not surprised that Gro was not better known in the United States. Gro matured politically as she dealt with a constant confrontation with the conservative leader Kåre Willoch. She eventually became a mother figure for Norway, as she became more secure in her position. Toward the end of her tenure as prime minister, Brundtland was criticized for standing above everyday politics, for not being seen as much in the Storting, and for too much international focus. One key to Brundtland's hold on power was that there was no real competition to her either inside or outside the Labor Party. Brundtland is extremely confident in her leadership, she had no need to prove anything, and she could no longer be called the "big mouth from Bygdøy." It was not easy to find anyone strongly opposed to her. Brundtland's success was due to her own skills plus timing and no strong opposition. Width could criticize only her environmental record in Norway, which he said was not impressive.[40]

According to Hanne Skartveit, Political Editor for *Verdens Gang*, Gro combined feminine and masculine styles of leadership. She was very much on her own level, unique, and even those who opposed her views respected her highly. Hers was a personality-driven success. She listened well and was open-minded. Brundtland's emotions were a problem at first but became less problematic later. She was definitely willing to use her power when necessary and could be very durable. She was very confident; she could cry at funerals and during her Christmas speeches, but she was powerful as well. She mixed her femininity with strength, redefining the common notion of strength perhaps. On the negative side, she could be an elitist, arrogant, short-tempered with reporters, and, as Strand noted, a poor public speaker. She had to balance environmental concerns with economic growth in Norway and was severely criticized by environmentalists. By 1995 Gro was untouchable politically in Norway, according to Skartveit.[41] The problem with Brundtland, according to some Norwegians, was that there were no opposition to her and too much consensus. I suppose it made Norwegians nervous. Politics were not supposed to be that carefree. I think that that sentiment expressed by many Norwegians points out something quite remarkable: Brundtland was able to lead so effectively that people noticed the "quietness." I would compare what these Norwegians were describing to the experience of leaving the busy city to hike in the woods—once you hike far enough, you rediscover quietness.

When asked how she managed such a difficult job and career with raising children, Brundtland said:

It was a big dilemma for me in 1974. Could I do it without taking away from my family and my role as mother? But to say no meant that women would be held back, because men do not say no to such opportunities when they have families. The first thing I did was to ask my husband. He said that he could do more.[42]

Gro announced her resignation on 23 October 1996 after dominating Norwegian politics for more than fifteen years. The 57-year-old prime minister gave no reason for stepping down but apparently had made the decision more than a year earlier. It was expected that she would step down, but her resignation came earlier than expected.[43]

VIGDIS FINNBOGADOTTIR

Vigdis was born in Reykjavik, the capital of Iceland, on 15 April 1930. Her father, Finnbogi Rutur, was an engineer and professor, and her mother, Sigridur Eiriksdottir, was the chair of the Icelandic Nurses' Association. Iceland was part of Denmark until 1944, when it once again became independent. Iceland was first settled and founded by Vikings in 874 and later came under control of both Norway and Denmark. Iceland had limited home rule from 1874 until after World War I, when it once again came under Danish rule. British forces occupied Iceland during World War II and were later replaced by American forces in 1944. Icelanders claimed independence from Denmark and declared Iceland a republic in 1944.

She left Iceland in 1949 to study French language and literature and drama at the University of Grenoble and at the Sorbonne in Paris. She later studied theater history in Denmark and French in Sweden. She rounded out her education at the University of Iceland. She was married in 1954 and divorced in 1963. She took a job as a teacher and used summers to guide tourists through Iceland. She eventually moved to the University of Iceland to teach French drama and later became a television personality. She was appointed director of the Reykjavik Theater Company in 1972. She was also named chair of the Advisory Committee on Cultural Affairs in the Nordic Countries.[44]

In 1975 the women of Iceland organized a general strike called "Women's Day Off," which nearly paralyzed the country.

In the capital city of Reykjavik, there were more than 20,000 women in the main square who had left their homes and told their husbands to take over. Men had to organize day care. Women's issues were spotlighted, and many Icelanders felt that it was time to have a woman leader. Vigdis was persuaded in 1980 to pursue the presidency. "Phone calls were coming from all over the country to urge me to run ... you do not see yourself as other people do. I was quite surprised that other people saw something in me that could be representative of Iceland," according to Vigdis.[45] Although she had never been active in politics, she was such a well-known television personality and cultural expert that many people supported her nomination. It was time, many supporters said, to prove that a woman could hold the office of president. She ran against three men. Many believed that her divorce and being a single parent might hurt her chances of being elected. She spent her four-month election campaign period crisscrossing the country and talking about cultural identity, history, and ecology. She was proud to claim that Iceland was the least polluted country in the world.

We have to be very much on our guard today. Iceland is less green than it was. There is erosion from wind and water and volcanic eruptions, so we are involved in reforestation programs, in sowing grass in the highlands. We need every green blade of grass to be able to feed humanity. It is a matter of not only protecting our own country, but also the countries of the world.[46]

Vigdis was elected president with 33.8 percent of the vote. The low percentage indicates that women in Iceland did not vote for her in droves. According to Vigdis, "Many ladies do not have confidence in themselves because in the male society they're used to having men run the whole thing. They don't have confidence in themselves, so why should they have confidence in another woman?"[47] The constitution of Iceland does not grant political responsibility to the president, and she has only limited governmental authority. Among her duties is the signing of all bills passed in the Parliament. "The President of Iceland is not a political person," she explains. "I've never been involved in politics or even belonged to any political party."[48]

Vigdis was inaugurated in August 1980 for a four-year term. She was the first popularly elected woman head of state (in contrast to heads of government like Thatcher and Gandhi). Icelandic presidents are required to sign all legislation passed by the Allthing, or Parliament (the oldest one in Europe). Although she had veto power, she never exercised it. Unlike many political leaders, Vigdis had an open door to the public. Twice a week, Icelanders were given ready access to her to discuss problems or just to talk. Her ability to bridge cultural differences was valuable in a meeting with British prime minister Margaret Thatcher in 1982. Previous to their meeting, England and Iceland had engaged in a fishing rights dispute known as the Cod War.

Vigdis believed that leadership was about

conviction, it's about vision, and it's about this longing, this wish to get your idea out ... leadership is all about this whole question of listening and then leading ... you don't go into politics to be loved. If you want to be loved you cultivate your family and friends. If you're really going to make decisions you're going to make some people angry .... Everybody likes approval. But you have to make decisions, you can't live with approval. You have to live with making the right decisions for the large majority of people.[49]

She decided to run for reelection in 1984 and had no real opposition. In 1986 Iceland received international attention when U.S. president Ronald Reagan and Soviet leader Mikhail Gorbachev chose Reykjavik for their summit. The summit was successful, and only two years later communism would fall in the Soviet Union.[50] Vigdis was reelected again in 1988 and 1992. She left office in 1996. Her legacy as the president of Iceland is as a cultural ambassador, unifier, and optimist.

We may only be 230,000 people in this country, but we run this society as if we were 2 million. We have television, radio, a national theater, a municipal theater, a symphony orchestra, and an opera ... we have everything. We have been investing, we have been energetic, and we are very independent. That's why I'm optimistic. If you're pessimistic it only slows you down.[51]

Vigdis stated at an International Women's Leadership Forum held in Stockholm in 1996:

Women cannot lead without men. They would always take men into consideration. ... [women's leadership] should not be viewed as exclusionary, but as an integral component leading toward a society in which a question of male and female leadership has become irrelevant .... Women's interest in democracy should not be confined to self-interest.[52]

Vigdis described her presidential victory as a milestone of equal rights for men and women.[53]

When asked if men go into politics for power, and women for influence on certain issues, Vigdis responded: "I have often asked myself and other people which do your prefer, which would you want, influence or power? And most of them their answer is influence because through influence you can get tremendous power ... we are all wishing people to go the path that we want to lead."[54] Vigdis believes that men and women have a similar way of governing because making a decision is always a very, very lonely job:

whatever advice you get you are alone to make the decision. And you are the only one who is responsible for the decision. So I don't think there is any difference; let's not forget that men are sensitive also. And it is difficult for them as well.[55]

Finnbogadottir left office in 1996 after serving Iceland for sixteen years as president. Her legacy continues to influence people both inside and outside Scandinavia. She is now an integral part of Harvard's John F. Kennedy School of Government Council of Women World Leaders. Although she was not a powerful political force in the traditional sense, she did have influence and provided an interesting example for future leadership studies.

VIOLETA BARRIOS DE CHAMORRO

Few national leaders have to face the dual challenges of economic development and healing a divided nation torn by civil war. Violeta Barrios de Chamorro not only faced these challenges as the newly elected president of Nicaragua in 1990 but did so as a woman leader in a political system dominated by men and the culture of machismo.[56] Her continuing struggle to bring peace and prosperity to Nicaragua through reconciliation has been a daunting task. Oddly enough, Chamorro's role as healer of her own family—where half were pro-Sandinista and half pro-contra—reflected in microcosm her role as healer of the nation.

The political history of Nicaragua has been characterized by invasions, civil wars, and coups d'etat. Democratic traditions have not been able to take root due to the debilitating effects of colonization by the Spanish in the sixteenth century and military intervention by the United States since the nineteenth century. Consequently, Nicaraguan political culture has been tainted by authoritarianism and dominance by the military.[57]

In the authoritarian tradition, the Somosa family ruled Nicaragua from 1937 to 1979. With the help of the United States, the Somosa dictatorships held a firm grip on Nicaragua and ignored basic human rights. In 1979 the Sandinista (Sandinista National Liberation Front, or FSLN) forces toppled the Somosas and promised a socialist restructuring of society. However, the Sandinistas, led by Daniel Ortega, could not completely consolidate their grip on the country before the old Somosa guard, under U.S. direction and with U.S. support, rose in armed opposition. These "contra" rebels began a bloody civil war that lasted until 1990, when Violeta Chamorro won the presidency and negotiated an end to the conflict. Chamorro came to power after one of the most free elections in Nicaraguan history. She set out to bring peace, prosperity, and reconciliation to a divided Nicaragua and had some early policy successes. She brought runaway inflation under control, cut the military by 75 percent, and demobilized the opposition contra rebels. She also restored basic political freedoms and human rights. However, Chamorro's power base began eroding in 1990. The electoral coalition that brought her to power began to abandon her. The Sandinistas, despite their retaining control of the military, police, and intelligence service, turned against Chamorro as well. To make matters worse, the United States stopped the disbursement of over $100 billion in aid to Nicaragua, largely due to the efforts of pro-contra U.S. senator Jesse Helms (R-North Carolina). Although the funds were eventually sent, the delay damaged the fragile Nicaraguan economy. The United States demanded that Chamorro sever her ties to the Sandinistas. U.S. officials seemed to miss the point that her ability to balance between the contra and Sandinista forces has been the only stopgap in the continuation of the civil war—a war that makes nation building impossible. Presently, the political climate in Nicaragua is explosive, and groups are fragmented. The once-strong coalition that brought Chamorro to power is gone.[58]

Violeta Chamorro came from a wealthy family and was sent to school in the United States in order to learn English. Not being terribly excited about school, she returned and married Pedro Joaquin Chamorro, the editor of the prominent anti-Somosa newspaper *La Prensa*. They were married for 27 years until his death in 1978. After his assassination in 1978, Violeta took over as editor of the paper. When the government of Anastasio Somosa fell to the Sandinistas in 1979, she served as the only woman member of the civilian junta that had provisional rule over Nicaragua after the revolution. Daniel Ortega was one of the other prominent members of the junta. She later said that she served because "they needed me ... they needed the name of my husband, and the name of *La Prensa* .... I wouldn't have been patriotic to refuse." Chamorro served on the junta for only a short time. Although she left the junta, officially citing health reasons, she later confided that she did not agree with the course the Sandinistas were taking—excessive militarism, increasing Cuban pressure, and a loss of interest in democratic ideals.[59]

The Sandinistas faced a serious challenge in consolidating their power in Nicaragua. The spirit of Somosa lived on in an opposition army made up of members of his former National

Guard. Contras planned a counterrevolution from staging sites in Honduras. They were then heavily supported by the United States under the leadership of U.S. president Ronald Reagan. The civil war waged on in the 1980s. The Sandinistas finally consolidated power in 1984, when Ortega was elected president, but the U.S.-supported contras kept the pressure on. Chamorro, in her position at *La Prensa*, protested the Sandinista's press censorship.[60] Yet, despite her opposition to the Sandinistas, Chamorro was not a puppet of the United States or a contra supporter. In a 1986 letter to Nicaraguan leader Daniel Ortega, she clarified her position:

How quickly you have forgotten my strong nationalist position. Remember that in 1979, in San José, Costa Rica, I was the only one who opposed any resolution of the Nicaraguan problem that included the involvement of foreign countries. What I said then I say now: the grave crisis afflicting Nicaragua must be resolved among ourselves, the Nicaraguans, without the interference of Cubans, Soviets or Americans.[61]

Throughout the 1980s, Chamorro continued her attacks against the human rights record of the Sandinistas. She insisted that Western democracies should demand a civilized government in Nicaragua, free elections, and human rights. Moreover, she began calling for a national dialogue and reconciliation between the warring contras and Sandinistas. Chamorro often called on the image of her martyr husband in her *La Prensa* editorials.[62] After the Sandinistas shut down the paper in 1986, Chamorro came out with an article in the U.S. journal *Foreign Affairs* that not only condemned the action but also made it clear that her opposition to the Sandinistas did not constitute approval of Reagan's policies. Again she called for a national dialogue to return Nicaragua to normalcy.[63] The paper was later reopened as defiant as ever—Chamorro's remained one of the principal voices against Sandinista rule. Her editorials were continually censored, and Sandinista mobs vandalized her home. In 1988 the Sandinistas began a propaganda campaign against her and *La Prensa*. They attempted to tie Chamorro to the U.S.-sponsored contras. The tactic did not work, and diverse anti-Sandinista groups came together under the Unión Nacional Opositora (UNO) party to name Violeta to unseat Ortega after his February 1989 announcement that the elections would be moved up to November 1989.[64] Ortega did this in exchange for the demobilization of the contras. These events were prompted by Costa Rican president Oscar Arias' leadership in formulating a peace accord among Central American countries. The goal was regional stability.

Chamorro claimed that she did not want the position of president, but the "people asked me to accept, and I did so gladly because the need in this country is so great." She centered her campaign on peace and reconciliation. Chamorro was compared to Aquino in the Philippines—she was considered brave, honest, and reliable. Her strong Catholic ties, like Aquino's, were apparent in her public speeches. In fact, once when asked to speak, she recited the Lord's Prayer. She also commanded the respect of those who held her husband in great esteem.[65]

The United States supported the Nicaraguan election efforts with $9 million in aid. Nearly $4 million of that money was earmarked for nonpartisan technical support of the electoral process. Some of this money went directly to the UNO. In spite of this U.S. support, the UNO was still short of cash, so Chamorro made trips abroad to get more support. There is some evidence to indicate that Venezuelan president Carlos Andrés Pérez funded the UNO as well. This would be no surprise since he was a longtime friend of Chamorro and had dispatched bodyguards to protect her and consultants to advise her on economic policy matters. Despite these efforts, by October 1989 it looked as though the FSLN and Ortega would win the election. The UNO campaign remained underfinanced and disorganized.[66]

Foreign representatives from the Organization of American States (OAS), the United Nations (UN), and former U.S. president Jimmy Carter observed the elections. The assumption by Ortega was that the FSLN would win in a fair contest. However, much to his surprise, Violeta Chamorro won with 54.7 percent of the vote. Many did not think she would win because of her lack of political experience. However, in her political naïveté, there was a refreshing feeling of honesty. She once said that "there's no need to study how to govern a country. ... I have accepted the challenge to revive my country with love and peace, according to the dictates of my conscience." Despite the UNO success, the FSLN remained the largest single party.[67] In the end, the FSLN reevaluated its party and principles. The Sandinistas discovered that they had placed too much emphasis on control and centralization of the public administration, that their policies were often implemented with coercion, that they confronted the Catholic Church too frequently, and that they disregarded the Indian peoples of the Atlantic coast. Ironically, the Sandinistas may have set the stage for Chamorro's coming to power by substantially increasing political opportunity for women after the 1979 revolution.[68]

Winning the election was one thing; effectively leading a war-torn country was another. Nicaragua and most of Central America were described by the International Commission for the Recovery and Development of Central America (the Sanford Commission) as trapped in a cycle of violence that impeded development. The resulting poverty, in turn, intensified the violence. The report outlined recommendations that included increasing social justice, democratic participation, and international development aid. Chamorro would have to achieve peace, stabilize the Nicaraguan economy, and institute democracy, while struggling to define her power base and fight for her political legitimacy.[69]

Chamorro took power on 25 April 1990 before several heads of state and both FSLN and UNO supporters. In her inaugural speech, President Chamorro said that one of her primary tasks was to "instill in all our actions the spirit of reconciliation." It was the first peaceful transition of power in Nicaraguan history. Although she named herself minister of defense, she retained Daniel Ortega's brother, General Humberto Ortega, as head of the army. This turned out to be a controversial move. Her strategy was to use Humberto to lessen Sandinista opposition to her new government. However, in protest, two of Chamorro's cabinet ministers resigned, and the contras threatened to resist the demobilization efforts. They did not understand that Chamorro was attempting to disarm the volatile political climate that bred the contra war by establishing a middle ground. In addition to the job of demobilizing the contra forces and downsizing the Sandinista army, she also faced a terrible economic crisis. Per capita income was at the same level as in 1950, and the inflation rate was 43 percent.[70] The ten-year contra war had crippled the Nicaraguan economy, and the subsequent U.S. embargo had been devastating. U.S. president George Bush was pleased in the change of leadership in Nicaragua but threatened to hold back $300 million in aid if he could not approve of Chamorro's political appointments. Despite these problems, it seemed as though the spirit of reconciliation was holding back the resumption of the civil war. As Chamorro put it: "Reconciliation is more beautiful than victory."[71]

As president, Chamorro has demonstrated a penchant for using powerful symbols. In addition to evoking her husband's image at every opportunity, on one occasion she arranged for 15,000 automatic rifles to be dumped into a pit and covered with concrete. It was a ceremonial "farewell to arms" signifying the end of the contra war.[72] In her first 100 days in office, Chamorro survived two general strikes, made progress in demobilizing the contras, and worked toward cooperation with the Sandinistas. The strikes were organized by the Sandinistas in protest of her economic austerity measures, which included layoffs, wage cuts, and attempts to sell state-owned companies. The contras also presented problems for Chamorro, as they formed an alliance with right-wing members of the UNO. In response, Chamorro negotiated a settlement and allotted contras land in demilitarized zones.[73]

Among all of these challenges, the economic crisis seemed to be the most daunting for the new president. The Sandinista government had turned over reserves of $3 billion, $13 billion in foreign debt, and an economic system that relied on a state-owned bank and over 400 state-owned companies. The Sandinistas retained control of the military, the police, and the trade unions.[74] Because of these facts, economic reform—including deficit-cutting measures, cutbacks in military spending, and privatization of industries—proved difficult. Chamorro did cut the defense budget from 25 percent of the total government budget to 16 percent, reducing the army from 96,000 men to 35,000. However, she also realized that too many cutbacks could lead to more general strikes—she had to explore other methods.[75]

Chamorro has been criticized as merely a figurehead. Upon assuming power, it was true that she had little knowledge of government and world affairs. She often forgot names of foreign leaders and struggled to remember well-known events (not unlike U.S. president Ronald Reagan). Real power in Nicaragua has been said to rest with her son-in-law, Antonio Lacayo, who served as her chief adviser and minister of the presidency. Lacayo often assumed the role of president when Chamorro was out of the country. Vice President Virgilio Godoy Reyes, who should have been the one to assume the office in Chamorro's absence, fell into disfavor. Godoy was a leading Sandinista critic and one of the most powerful men in the Nicaraguan right-wing. He has been accused of stirring up the recontras in efforts to undermine Chamorro's authority.[76]

It became clear to Chamorro that there were many problems with the Sandinista-dominated police and the remaining contras. Peaceful political transitions were new in Nicaragua, where politics had been characterized by a "winner-take-all" mentality—the losers either died or moved to Miami.[77] To meet Nicaragua's serious problems, the Chamorro government experimented with a method of national consensus-building through negotiation, known as *concertación*, or national dialogue. Beginning in August 1990, Chamorro worked with businesses and workers to form a consensus on an economic program. The FSLN sought to protect the gains they had made in the revolution in terms of agrarian reform and nationalization of important industries. UNO leaders wanted privatization and the return of confiscated property. Remarkably, such a consensus was reached and approved by the National Assembly in 1990. The plan allowed Chamorro to go out and seek foreign aid donors. Unfortunately, a renewed crisis in the rural areas erupted by the end of the year, threatening the newly forged consensus. Stability seemed elusive, but Chamorro insisted that only through bargaining, compromise, and negotiation (*concertación*) could Nicaragua's problems be solved.[78]

In 1991 Chamorro was besieged by political forces on all sides, despite her being loved by most Nicaraguans. Political opponents had trouble adapting to a woman and mother figure in power. One opposition official said that it was hard to criticize her because she was a woman. Her disarming demeanor also caught some politicians off guard (i.e., calling advisers "my love"). Labor groups affiliated with the FSLN seized new freedoms and, according to the president, "invented new ways almost everyday to go on strike." She stressed that time was needed to heal the country.[79] Chamorro did make some headway with her trip to the United States in April 1991. She was able to clear up a $360 million World Bank debt with President Bush's help. In spite of Sandinista-led strikes and contra land seizures, Chamorro seemed to have established some type of equilibrium in Nicaragua.[80]

By 1992 Nicaragua was on the road to recovery but was little noticed by the world. Chamorro seemed to realize that increased trade would revive the Nicaraguan economy faster than foreign aid. Bowing to the Nicaraguan right-wing and the United States, Chamorro announced the return of Sandinista-confiscated property in September 1992. Heeding U.S. secretary of state James Baker, who warned Chamorro of the importance of security for investors, she also fired several Sandinista police officials. This move was tied to the freeing up of $104 million in U.S. aid.[81]

U.S. government interest in Nicaraguan affairs is not new. Pressure from the United States to mold Nicaraguan politics has existed ever since the proclaiming of the Monroe Doctrine in 1823. In 1855 William Walker was sent to Managua by U.S. businessman Cornelius Vanderbilt in order to help overthrow the government of Fruto Chamorro (an ancestor of Pedro Joaquin Chamorro). During the height of the Cold War in the 1980s, U.S. interest in Nicaragua did not diminish. Even after the end of the

Cold War, right-wing forces in the United States kept up the pressure. Senator Helms has spearheaded the Cold War struggle in Nicaragua. It has been said that "Helms will not rest until every Sandinista official is gone." However, he does not like Chamorro either. After Chamorro agreed to firing certain Sandinista police officials in exchange for the freeing up of U.S. aid money, Helms effectively stopped the aid anyway, calling the Chamorro government a band of "terrorists, thugs, thieves, and murderers."[82]

At the end of 1992 Chamorro found that the recontras were gaining strength in the countryside. Reconciliation was hard to achieve in the rural areas, where personal and political vendettas often mixed and where much of the population remained heavily armed. During the election, the UNO promised the contras that they would be resettled and protected from Sandinista retributions. But by 1992 there had been numerous political murders on both sides—180 to 200 contras and 100 Sandinistas had been killed.[83]

In 1993 Chamorro shifted her power base from the center-right coalition that elected her to a center-left coalition with the Sandinistas. She did this in concert with her renewed efforts to combat Nicaragua's social problems. The tough economic austerity measures, undertaken since her election to right the economy, proved too difficult for the poor and rural workers. She called 1993 the year to reactivate the economy with a social consciousness. Chamorro wanted to place special emphasis on health, education, housing, and unemployment—areas that had worsened under her rule. The right-wing members of the UNO were left out in this new strategy. Chamorro's decision to form the center-left alliance may have been prompted by former contra leader Alfredo César, who had been a problem for Chamorro for some time.[84] In 1992 he had accused her of betraying democracy when she did not heed his policy advice. He also teamed up with Senator Helms to cut U.S. aid to Chamorro. Apparently, César and the Nicaraguan ambassador in Washington had fed Helms' staff with negative information on Chamorro's administration that ultimately led to the U.S. Senate's cutting off aid to

Nicaragua. In trying to stay in the middle and keep forces at the extremes from gaining too much control, Chamorro was forced to shift her power base on each major issue and therefore had difficulty keeping political allies.[85]

The increasingly right-wing UNO coalition stepped up its efforts to destabilize Chamorro's administration in 1993. Alfredo César was accused by General Humberto Ortega of stirring up armed recontras in the mountains of northern Nicaragua, with the idea of keeping the country in turmoil and making Chamorro's government collapse. Ortega said that the government's economic program was stifled by pressure in the northern agricultural areas, where the recontras were active. Some of the rebels in the north robbed banks and distributed money to the peasants (à la Robin Hood). In February 1993, UNO deputy Humberto Castilla made a trip to the United States and returned with a message from Senator Helms, telling the recontras of his pride in their struggle for freedom. Although the UNO supported Chamorro's free market policies, it could not tolerate her working and compromising with the Sandinistas.[86] Chamorro renewed her efforts at reaching a national accord in May 1993. She met with all sides—seven leading political organizations, private sector groups, and trade unions. She called on the diverse groups to work together in providing political stability, arguing that instability was hurting all factions because foreign investors were not forthcoming.[87]

In August 1993 a renewed conflict between the recontras and the Sandinistas led to two hostage crises. On 19 August a group of recontras kidnapped a delegation of government officials who had been sent to the northern region for peace talks. The group demanded the resignation of General Ortega. In retaliation, a Sandinista commando team seized UNO headquarters in Managua on 20 August and took UNO leader Alfredo César prisoner. These events came shortly after President Chamorro and the National Assembly approved a controversial amnesty bill for the recontras. This amnesty came in the wake of banditry in the north, where jobs are scarce. The recontras rejected the bill, saying that they did nothing wrong to be given amnesty for. The UNO then called for shortening Chamorro's term in office.[88]

The kidnapping crises ultimately came to a peaceful end. Chamorro hailed it as a victory for dialogue and reconciliation. However, in trying to pursue a course of reconciliation, Chamorro found herself between two very intolerant groups, both willing to turn on her.[89] Having averted the hostage crises, Chamorro faced increasing pressure from U.S. State Department officials to oust more Sandinistas. The United States even suggested that the Nicaraguan government was tied to terrorism.[90] Additionally, Chamorro's critics pointed out that the hostage crises were resolved while she was out of the country. This gave credence to the idea that Lacayo was the real power in Nicaragua.[91]

In September 1993, showing signs of moving her power base to the right again, Chamorro made the decision to fire army chief General Humberto Ortega and put military intelligence under civilian rule. Rumors of his firing had been circulating since October 1992.[92] The general's brother, Daniel Ortega, responded by telling Chamorro: "You are not the owner of the country." However, the move was applauded by both the UNO and the U.S. government. U.S. secretary of state Warren Christopher stated that the shift toward civilian rule of the military would free up an additional $98 million in aid to Nicaragua. Chamorro faced tremendous difficulty trying to push for reconciliation amid economic chaos and political intrigue. Senator Helms' efforts to disrupt Chamorro's reconciliation program remained devastating. The Nicaraguans needed U.S. and other foreign aid, but such aid was tied to moving further away from the Sandinistas. Firing General Ortega was difficult because Chamorro had always seen him as a stabilizing pillar in her government. He was important in reducing the military and gave her policies a sense of legitimacy with the Sandinistas. By the fall of 1993 economic measures had stabilized the currency, inflation was down to 3.5 percent from 43 percent in 1990, but growth was still nonexistent, and unemployment was at 60 percent. Political instability and economic stagnation fed each other and discouraged foreign investors. Without investors, poverty and instability increased, thereby creating a vicious cycle. Some moderate Sandinistas conceded that perhaps the time had come for General Ortega to go, but they also noted that U.S. senator Helms should be kept out of Nicaraguan affairs in the future.[93]

In November 1993 the Sandinistas pressured Chamorro to reform the economic decision-making powers of the president. In fact, there were charges that the Sandinistas were staging crises in order to paralyze Chamorro's goverment.[94] Most economic decisions had been made secretly between the government and the International Monetary Fund (IMF). The Sandinistas wanted to reform the constitution to prohibit the reelection of the president, subordinate the army to even more civilian control, and provide for a less partisan judiciary. In retaliation, Chamorro threatened to resign if anything other than minor changes were made to the constitution.[95]

In January 1994 Chamorro announced her intent to readdress the problems of the poor in Nicaragua. The economic measures under her tenure in office had not necessarily helped the poor. She promised that in 1994 the government would support the small farmer. These policies were part of a new grassroots effort to build a social agenda that would respond to the economic demands of the rural poor living in communities where the recontras had been using banditry to win their allegiance. The trouble was that social reform at the grassroots level tended to jeopardize the loan deals worked out with the IMF and World Bank.[96]

Overall, criticism of Chamorro has centered on her lack of political experience and reliance on her husband's image: "Violeta Chamorro's status in Nicaraguan society is largely ascriptive ... yet she achieved the ultimate status that a woman can attain in Nicaraguan society by being the devout widow of a politically correct martyr."[97] However, she has not necessarily been a model for feminists interested in getting more women into positions of political power. During her presidential campaign she asserted, "I'm not a feminist. ... I am a woman dedicated to my home, as Pedro has taught me." She has not favored increasing the participation of women in politics and has given few political appointments to women.[98] In spite of that, at least one other woman in Central America has been inspired to run for presidential office—Margairita Penón de Arias, wife of former Costa Rican president Oscar Arias.[99] Chamorro has been forced to walk a tortuous path between renewed civil war and economic ruin. Her term ended in 1996. Her time in office was testimony to her ability to weather severe crises. Whether the opposition forces will be able to resolve their differences through peaceful means remains to be seen.

SUMMARY

The three women chosen for this comparison share some leadership attributes and differ on many others. Interestingly, all three leaders left office in 1996. Finnbogadottir began her tenure in office in 1980, sooner than the others. Brundtland had her first tenure in office in 1981, and Chamorro in 1990. All three were considered mother figures in their respective countries—Chamorro the most so, then Brundtland, followed by Finnbogadottir. To some degree, the three women reflected their nations more than their gender. Chamorro did not call herself a feminist, and Brundtland and Finnbogadottir did not overly emphasize feminism but worked toward the greater good in keeping with their Scandinavian egalitarian traditions. Brundtland was perhaps the most accomplished politician among the three, having served in a government post and in the Parliament prior to her service as prime minister. Chamorro's husband and Brundtland's father were politically connected. Finnbogadottir was not politically connected through her family. In terms of education, Chamorro was the least educated, Brundtland the most (being a physician). All three adapted well to the political realities of their respective countries and regions. All were from wealthy families. All three were considered unifiers, cultural ambassadors, and optimists. Chamorro had the most difficult go of it, by far. Her ability to find equilibrium was remarkable. Brundtland changed Norwegian politics dramatically. She ultimately centered the left-leaning social democrats and grabbed a large and loyal constituency throughout the country. No one in Norwegian politics had ever had such a grip on power. Finnbogadottir, being in a largely ceremonial position, did not wield power in a direct way. Her influence in Iceland was more indirect. The comparison shows that factors other than gender seemed to influence these leaders in their terms of service.

NOTES

1. There were very nearly three, but Elisabeth Rehn of Finland lost in a close election in February 1994.

2. Gloria Steinem, "Gro Harlem Brundtland," *Ms* (January 1988), 74.

3. Some theorists go as far as to say that power has shifted to the private sector so that women could more easily gain public power—the shrinking institutions theory.

4. Richard E. Matland, "The World's Leader in Female Representation: Norway" in Shin-wha Lee, ed., *International Directory of Women's Political Leadership, 1991-92* (College Park, MD: Center for Political Leadership and Participation, 1992), pp. 163-67.

5. Steinar Hansson and Ingolf Håkon Teigene, *Makt og Mannefall: Historien om Gro Harlem Brundtland* (Oslo: J.W. Cappelens Forlag, 1992), p. 7.

6. Hansson and Teigene, pp. 27-28.

7. Hansson and Teigene, 31; Olga S. Opfell, *Women Prime Ministers and Presidents* (Jefferson, NC: McFarland, 1993), pp. 101-2.

8. Opfell, 104; Pranay Gupte, "OPEC's Scandinavian Partner," *Forbes* (15 December 1986), 146.

9. Steinem, p. 75.

10. Opfell, p. 104; Hansson and Teigene, p. 38; Nancy Gibbs, "Norway's Radical Daughter," *Time* (25 September 1989), 42.

11. Hansson and Teigene, pp. 11-13; Opfell, p. 104.

12. Hansson and Teigene, pp. 14-15. She turned some heads when once she opened a Labor Party meeting by reading the position in a dialect not generally used by the power elite in Norway—Nynorsk.

13. Opfell, p. 105.

14. Hansson and Teigene, pp. 16-17.

15. Hansson and Teigene, pp. 20-21.

16. Hansson and Teigene, pp. 24-25.

17. Hansson and Teigene, p. 50; Opfell, p. 105.

18. Hansson and Teigene, pp. 51-52, 75-76.

19. Opfell, p. 105.

20. Hansson and Teigene, pp. 113-14, 116; Jostein Nyhamar, *Arbeiderbevegelsens Historie i Norge* (Oslo: Arbeiderbevegelsen, 1990), pp. 348-353, 451; *Arbeiderbladet*, 31 January 1981, p. 1; *Arbeiderbladet*, 31 December 1992, p. 25; Tone Kraft, "Brundtland," *Norseman*, no. 2 (1981), 28-30.

21. Nyhamar, pp. 447-48.

22. Hansson and Teigene, pp. 121-22; Opfell, pp. 105-6.

23. Steinem, p. 75.

24. Opfell, p. 106.

25. The women in Norway first voted in 1913. In 1921 the first woman was elected to the Storting. From 1945 to 1957 only 6 percent of the Storting were women, 10 percent in 1960, 20 percent in 1970, and 34 percent in 1985. Nyhamar, pp. 505, 515; Opfell, pp. 107-8; Gupte, p. 146; *Time* (6 October 1986), 40.

26. Even though women have made great strides in the public sector leadership, only 7.2 percent of university professors are women, and only 3.3 percent of corporate leaders are women. Even the civil service seems resistant to the same change that political office has seen—only 10 percent of senior civil service employees are women. Looking at the reasons for success in getting women into positions of political leadership—like proportional representation, multiparty competition, a receptive political culture based on social justice, equality, and solidarity, or the political activism of a relatively strong women's movement—reveals that such factors do not translate well into the private sector. Hege Skjeie, "The Uneven Advance of Norwegian Women," *New Left Review* 187 (May/June 1991), 79.

27. For more information on the balancing of security interests in Scandinavia, see Bruce O. Solheim, *The Nordic Nexus: A Lesson in Peaceful Security* (Westport, CT: Praeger Publishers, 1994).

28. Gro Harlem Brundtland, "Global Change and Our Common Future," *Environment* 31 (June 1989), 43.

29. Opfell, p. 108; Gupte, p. 146; *Time* (6 October 1986), 40; Gibbs, pp. 43-44.

30. Gro Harlem Brundtland, "Global energipolitkk. Et norsk syn," *Internasjonal Politikk*, nos. 5-6 (1987), 34.

31. Gibbs, p. 42.

32. Opfell, pp. 110-11.

33. Fred Hauptfuhrer, "On Top of the World," *People* (20 April 1987), 38.

34. Gibbs, p. 44.

35. Gupte, p. 146; Gibbs, p. 44.

36. Bill Moyers, *A World of Ideas with Bill Moyers*, "Changing Agendas with Gro Harlem Brundtland" videotape (Public Affairs Television, New York, 1990).

37. Hege Skjeie, "Politisk Lederskap," *Nytt Norsk Tidsskrift* (2/1992), 123-26.

38. Skjeie, "Politisk Lederskap," pp. 126, 132-133.

39. Arne Strand, Deputy Chief Editor, *Arbeiderbladet,* Oslo, Norway, and former State Secretary for Prime Minister Gro Harlem Brundtland, 1987-1989. Interview, conducted on 3 July 1995 in Oslo.

40. Henrik Width, Political Editor, *Aftenposten*, Oslo, Norway. Interview, conducted 27 June 1995 in Oslo.

41. Hanne Skartveit, Political Editor, *Verdens Gang (VG)*, Oslo, Norway. Interview, conducted 29 June 1995 in Oslo.

42. Kirsten K. Berentsen, "Drivkraften bak Gro," *Magasinet SAS Norge*, no. 4 (Summer 1995), 9.

43. Gro Harlem Brundtland, *Mitt Liv, 1939-1986* (Oslo, Norway: Gyldendal, 1997), pp. 7-17.

44. Alida Brill, ed., *A Rising Public Voice: Women in Politics Worldwide* (New York: Feminist Press, 1995), p. 141.

45. Bernhardt J. Hurwood, "Iceland's Optimist." *Christian Science Monitor,* 16 September 1982, p. 15.

46. Opfell, p. 98.

47. Hurwood, p. 15.

48. Brill, p. 141; Hurwood, p. 15.

49. Council of Women World Leaders, 1998 Summit of the Council of Women World Leaders at the John F. Kennedy School of Government, Harvard University. Transcript located at the following website:http://www.ksg.harvard.edu/ksgpress/ksg_news/transcripts/ cwwl. htm.

50. Opfell, pp. 95-100.

51. Hurwood, p. 15.

52. Elizabeth Pond, "Women in Leadership: A Letter from Stockholm." *The Washington Quarterly* 19, no. 4 (Autumn 1996), 60.

53. *Christian Science Monitor*, "New Heroine for Icelandic Saga," 2 July 1980, p. 24.

54. Council of Women World Leaders, 1998 Summit.

55. Council of Women World Leaders, 1998 Summit.

56. The Spanish conquistadores imported machismo—an exaggerated sense of maleness and aggressiveness. It is sometimes known as the cult of virility.

57. Michelle A. Saint-Germaine, "Women in Power in Nicaragua: Myth and Reality," in Michael A. Genovese, ed. *Women as National Leaders* (London: Sage Publications, 1993), pp. 71-74.

58. *Christian Science Monitor*, 26 August 1993; Opfell, p. 169; Saint-Germaine, p. 75.

59. Patricia Taylor Edmisten, *Nicaragua Divided: La Prensa and the Chamorro Legacy* (Pensacola: University of West Florida Press, 1990), pp. 72, 91; Richard L. Millet, "Nicaragua: A Glimmer of Hope?" *Current History* 89 (January 1990), 36; Opfell, pp. 173-175; Saint-Germaine, pp. 78-79.

60. Opfell, p. 176.

61. Edmisten, p. 92.

62. Edmisten, pp. 94-95.

63. Violeta Barrios de Chamorro, "The Death of La Prensa," *Foreign Affairs* 65, no. 2 (Winter 1986/87), 384, 386.

64. The UNO was a coalition of fourteen parties that had a mandate for change. These parties individually did not account for more than 6 percent of the seats eventually allotted in the National Assembly. The FSLN was by far the dominant single party.

65. Opfell, pp. 176-77; Edmisten, pp. 102-3; *Vogue*, August 1990, 385-86; Saint-Germaine, pp. 80-87. Chamorro's popularity with the general public was astonishing. She was called the "Virgin of Nicaragua." Some poor Nicaraguans believed that if they touched her dress, they would be healed. She explained that this "terrified me" (*Vogue*, August 1990, p. 386).

66. Saint-Germaine, p. 90; Millet, p. 36.

67. The most popular theme in the UNO campaign was to end the military draft. The FSLN campaign slogan of "all will be better" did not fare as well as the UNO slogan: "UNO! Yes, it can change things."

68. Opfell, p. 177; McCoy, pp. 117-18; Saint-Germaine, pp. 81-82, 87.

69. Saint-Germaine, pp. 87-88.

70. McCoy, pp. 118-19.

71. *New York Times*, 27 April 1990, p. A35; *Los Angeles Times*, 27 April 1990, p. B8; *Christian Science Monitor*, 27 April 1990, p. 3; *Christian Science Monitor*, 2 May 1990, p. 19.

72. Opfell, p. 178.

73. Opfell, p. 179.

74. *Los Angeles Times*, 19 July 1990, p. A4; *Washington Post*, 7 August 1990, p. A8.

75. *Christian Science Monitor*, 10 May 1990, p. 1; *Los Angeles Times*, 19 May 1990, p. A8; *New York Times*, 17 June 1990, sec. 1, p. 9.

76. Saint-Germaine, pp. 94-95. Oddly enough, the dispute between Chamorro and Godoy may have begun over office space. Chamorro even banned Godoy from the presidential office building. The UNO coalition may have won the election, but they were by no means a "happy family."

77. *Christian Science Monitor*, 14 December 1990, p. 7.

78. Opfell, pp. 178-79; McCoy, pp. 120, 132; *Wall Street Journal*, 17 December 1990, p. A8.

79. *New York Times*, 12 April 1991, p. A1.

80. *Christian Science Monitor*, 25 April 1991, p. 4.

81. *Christian Science Monitor*, 10 March 1992, p. 18; and 10 September 1992, p. 3.

82. Saint-Germaine, p. 72; *Christian Science Monitor*, 17 September 1992, p. 18.

83. *Washington Post*, 15 November 1992, p. A31.

84. César has been both a Sandinista and a contra and is not fully trusted by either side. He is also the brother-in-law of Antonio Lacayo.

85. *Washington Post*, 2 September 1992, p. A20; *New York Times*, 3 September 1992, p. A3, and 11 September 1992, p. A4; *Wall Street Journal*, 14 September 1992, p. A10; *Christian Science Monitor*, 12 January 1993.

86. *Washington Post*, 8 February 1993, p. A1.

87. *Washington Post*, 9 May 1993, p. A29.

88. *Washington Post*, 19 August 1993, p. A22, and 22 August 1993, p. A1; *New York Times*, 23 August 1993, p. A1; *Christian Science Monitor*, 23 August 1993.

89. *Christian Science Monitor*, 28 August 1993.

90. *Washington Post*, 22 August 1993, p. A29.

91. *Los Angeles Times*, 27 August 1993, p. A1.

92. *New York Times*, 29 October 1992, p. A3.

93. Newspapers in the United States seemed to carry gloomy forecasts for Chamorro's government in 1993. *Los Angeles Times*, 27 August 1993, p. A1; *New York Times*, 4 September 1993, p. 3; *Chris-*

tian Science Monitor, 10 September 1993; *Seattle Times*, 27 September 1993.

94. *Wall Street Journal*, 10 December 1993, p. A15.
95. *Christian Science Monitor*, 24 November 1993.
96. *Christian Science Monitor*, 9 February 1994.
97. Saint-Germaine, p. 80.
98. Saint-Germaine, p. 97.
99. Saint-Germaine, p. 100.

Chapter 4

Conclusion and Direction for Further Research

> Wathinth' abafazxi, wathinth' imbhokoto, basopha uzokufa! (Now you have touched the women, you have struck a rock)
> —South African women's antiapartheid anthem

> We can establish no real trust between nations until we acknowledge the power of love above all the other powers.
> —Eleanor Roosevelt, 1938

> War is simply not an acceptable way of resolving disputes.
> —Jeanette Rankin, First Woman in U.S. Congress

The world is being subjected to simultaneous and contradictory forces of fragmentation and integration. At a time when it is clear that we need each other to solve problems that recognize no boundaries or borders, we are dividing into ever smaller groups and battling one another. The gender war is but one of the fronts in this conflict. There is a tendency for many to believe that only women are interested in studies about women in politics—this type of assumption is evident in many other articles and books. This assumption is elitist and self-defeating. Being bogged down in equality-difference debates is also nonproductive. We need to achieve consensus of structure, not of content. I call this concept cooperation through diversity. We can use our individual strengths and differences to better the whole of society. Diversity and differences are strengths if people work together. An analogy would be helpful in illustrating how cooperation through diversity works. Imagine a hand. Each finger has the capability to move independently of the others, adjusting its movement forward and backward, up and down. Yet each of the five fingers is attached to the palm, which simultaneously allows for this articulation and provides the security of a base. Sometimes the fingers move individually, and sometimes together—each responding differently to stimuli that it encounters in the environment, yet each remaining attached to the palm. Were it not for the palm, the fingers would fling off into five different directions, and nothing would be accomplished. Were it not for the ability of the fingers to exercise flexibility, the hand would be stiff and useless. One finger or thumb alone cannot do the whole job. Even though the thumb is powerful, it needs the other fingers to grasp something and to create something. Likewise, the delicate nature of the small finger alone is weak, but it adds subtlety to the overall effect when used together with the others.[1]

The best way to understand the differences and similarities between men and women is to realize that we differ more as individuals than as genders. By understanding and comprehending individual differences, looking at how communities act, then regions, then nations, then the global body politic—only then can we come together and turn our differences into strengths and elements of cooperation, rather than into points of conflict.[2]

Many people find it disturbing that the gains achieved in 1992 in terms of the number of women in office have slipped. We seem to have moved beyond the trendiness of voting for a woman to wanting to vote for the best candidate. Individuals and their styles and leadership qualities are separate from their gender. Take a hypothetical situation: two women emerge as leaders. One woman is basically outgoing, extroverted, a military veteran, comes from a single parent family that was working-class poor, and now has five children in addition to being a political leader. The other woman is more introverted, aloof, from a rich family, a sheltered existence, not married, no children. It stands to reason that these two women may employ different leadership styles, and what they have to offer may be different based on their different individual experiences and personality types despite the fact that they are both women.

That having been said, we know that there are major influences on the person who becomes a leader, gender being only one of them, but there is also the basic personality or genetic character that scientists now believe we are born with. There are also the experiences that we have as individuals as we grow based on gender, environment, and family structure, and then there is something I call the will to power or why a person wants to be a leader. These four influences determine the leadership style a person employs. They are shown in Figure 4.1.

I have shown that of the two basic leadership styles, empowering and hierarchical, women seem to employ empowering more than men do. I have also added a leadership style, a hybrid situational empowering style. These leaders have a tendency to employ one type most of the time but switch to the other style under certain circumstances. Because few women have risen to top political positions in the world, their performance and the impact their leadership had on society constitute unique and valuable lines of inquiry. The emergence of women in such top positions may be both an effect and a cause of social change in the world and may signal that the tide has turned in the distribution of power between men and women.[3]

If gender affects style of leadership, then it would be most evident in the highest positions of government. One does not have to go back very far in time to study female heads of state. Only recently have women been elected into such positions. Women have, however, been active in the political process for some time, but top leadership positions have been denied to them. How would the world fare with women in charge? Essentialist theorists hold that women would promote nonviolent, caring, nurturing, and nonoppressive societies—feminist values would reduce militarism and strive for greater humanism.[4] Women leaders cannot escape the perceptions of most people that gender differences matter in leadership. A woman leader must therefore carry out the ordinary functions of her office and constantly prove her legitimate use of power. For those who would argue that women do not matter in politics, it is hard to justify the scholarly attention women are receiving. It follows that studying women at the top should reveal gender differences in leadership style more easily than studying other lower-level positions.[5]

Figure 4.1
The Making of a Leader

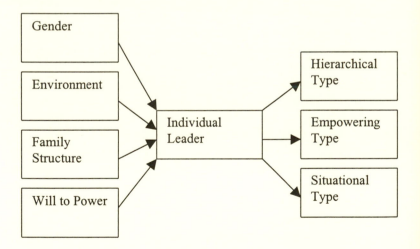

The women chosen for this study came from different political environments and cultural experiences. One thing that they have in common is that they made it to the top in spite of gender bias that exists around the world. The very fact that women have made it to the top indicates that a social change has already occurred. A woman leader who succeeds will begin to remove negative stereotypes for women. One who fails will reinforce them. By studying these women leaders, perhaps a new understanding will emerge regarding leadership itself.[6]

Some political analysts have pointed out an "appendage syndrome" involving women's coming to power. Accordingly, women such as Aquino of the Philippines, Bhutto of Pakistan, and Chamorro could not have ascended to the top without the reputation of their famous husbands or fathers. The criticism is that the symbology of power provided by their famous male relatives is not enough to lead. Someone who is held as the mother of a nation has a large responsibility. If such leaders fail, the failure seems worse than with a male leader. They are elected on emotional grounds instead of their political savvy. Two aspects of this observation that are disturbing. First, men who have come to power often have family ties to power, but nothing is made of that (e.g., John F. Kennedy). The classic double standard is applied to women who have famous relatives, but not to men. Second, even if one believes that a woman's only claim to power is through her famous male relative, once she is in power, she stands alone. A good example of this is Indira Gandhi of India. For sixteen years she proved herself to be the most formidable prime minister India has ever had.[7]

Women's history has gone through various stages. Gerda Lerner notes that the first historians dealing with women went about their work with "missionary zeal." There was a tendency to praise everything women did under oppression. Mary Beard challenged this dominant view in the 1930s in America when she wrote that women should not be noted for their being an oppressed group but that they have made a continuous and important contribution throughout history. This contribution, however, did not fit into the value system of historians who decided what was important to record. Lerner calls for studies on women to:

1. examine how women function differently in society than men do,
2. examine the different roles women have,
3. discard the oppressed group model,

4.   address the problem of women's education,
5.   distinguish for any given period what was considered a woman's place, and what her actual status was, and
6.   develop more equitable scales to determine the importance of women.[8]

Women's contributions have been different from, but equal to, men's.

DO WOMEN MAKE A DIFFERENCE?

Early studies have shown that the increased number of women in government in Norway have put some important issues on the political agenda and brought about some reforms. Between 1973 and 1977, 20 percent of the issues that women politicians raised concerned woman's rights and benefits, compared to only 4 percent of the same issues that were raised by men. More attention was paid to child care, widows' pensions, equal pay, assistance for single parents and for married women to join the workforce, and reduced working hours for parents.[9] Fewer roads were built in Norway after the percentage of women leaders reached 30 percent. These women leaders also appear to be influential in doubling the number of kindergartens, increasing the number and size of playgrounds, and allocating 90 percent of the new budget toward health and social sectors of the economy.[10]

Women leaders in Norway want to make changes and make a difference, but at the same time they do not want to act that differently than men do. Women politicians are generally more willing than men to cooperate across party lines on specific issues, but they still remain loyal in the end to their parties. This has led to a change in Parliament, where there are now more such examples of interparty cooperation and successful alliances, especially on women's issues. Nearly all Parliament members believe that women have reshaped Norway's national agenda. There is a much stronger emphasis on child care, health, education and family, the environment, and disarmament.[11]

The high number of women in politics in Norway has also changed people's attitudes toward women as leaders. A television debate on the European Union membership in Norway featured Brundtland with two other party leaders, Anne Enger Lahnstein and Kaci Kullman Five. Norwegians did not see three women talking; instead, they saw three politicians discussing the issues. Most Norwegians have moved beyond the novelty of having so many women in power. One exception may be that women politicians tend to call each other by first names, which is unusual among male politicians.

This book has looked at some results of female power. One of the most important is parental leave. Five years ago, parental leave in Norway was 20 weeks. It is now 35 weeks with full pay or 44 weeks with 80 percent pay. Women in power in Norway have successfully fended off the trend toward dismantling the social welfare system and have balanced social welfare with economic growth policies.

There is still work to be done in Norway. Women still do almost twice the housework, they earn only 80 percent of what men earn, only 52 percent of women work full-time, single motherhood is increasing, and only 23 percent of management positions in the labor market are held by women. Women are still increasingly the victims of sexual violence and harassment.[12]

This book set out to answer the following questions concerning female political leadership:

1. Is there a female style of nonaggressive leadership that relies on a power-sharing strategy rather than power-wielding one?
2. Does this style apply only to women?
3. Would women leaders promote peace and social justice better than their male counterparts have done in the past?

In response to the first and second questions, I believe that there is a style of nonaggressive, power-sharing leadership, but it appears not to be totally dependent on gender. Women seem to employ this style more than men, but men are also able to utilize it. The key is that this style of leadership has not been appreciated in the past, whether wielded by men or women. In response to the third question, having women more represented in world political leadership can only improve the chances for peace and social justice. This would free up the pool of good leaders who have been underutilized due to their style of leadership or just to the fact of their being women. The style of leadership, I believe, is more important than the gender of the leader in promoting peace and social justice.

What has been learned? We looked at only one political system and only three women leaders. When other women leaders are considered, one can see that most of them come from less developed nations. Most of these leaders appeared in democratic societies, and most came to power during times of distress. See the Appendix for the complete list. It would be important to assess the impact of male and female leaders who employ a more power-sharing type of leadership. This assessment should be cross-cultural. Perhaps societies turn to their women when the chips are down and neglect them when the good times are rolling. These topics may be the subjects for other books.

NOTES

1. Bruce O. Solheim, *The Nordic Nexus: A Lesson in Peaceful Security* (Westport, CT: Praeger, 1994), pp. 141-42.

2. As Buckminster Fuller once said: "I am not a category, a noun, or a thing, I am a verb." These are words to live by.

3. Michael A. Genovese, ed., *Women as National Leaders* (London: Sage Publications, 1993), p. 3.

4. Margarita Papandreou, "Feminism and Political Power: Some Thoughts on a Strategy for the Future," in Ellen Boneparth and Emily Stoper, eds. *Women, Power and Policy: Toward the Year 2000.* 2nd ed. (New York: Pergamon Press, 1988), pp. xi-xix.

5. Genovese, pp. 5-8.

6. Genovese, pp. 8-11.

7. Genovese, p. 5; Howard G. Chua-Eaon, "All in the Family," *Time* (Fall 1990), 33-34.

8. Gerda Lerner, "New Approaches to the Study of Women in American History," *Journal of Social History* 3, no. 1 (Fall 1969), 54-55, 60-62.

9. Marit Tovsen, "Women in Politics in Norway." Seminar paper for Women from Eastern Europe, Denmark, 19 August 1992, mimeograph, pp. 11-12.

10. Norwegian Labor Party Women's Movement, "Kvinner og makt," Ny hverdag, Kvinnepolitisk handlingsprogram, March 1985, p. 19.

11. Tovsen, pp. 12-13.

12. Tovsen, pp. 13-14.

Appendix: Comparison of Women National Leaders

Appendix
Comparison of Women National Leaders

	Country	Years in Office	Year of Enfran- chisement	% of Women in Legislature (1991)	Development Status of Country	Title	% of Women in Cabinet (1991)
Aquino, Corazon	Philippines	1986-92	1939	9.8	developing	P	4.0
Bandaranaike, Sirimavo	Sri Lanka	1960-65 1970-77	1931	4.2	developing	PM	4.2
Barbara, Agatha	Malta	1982-87				P	
Bhutto, Benazir	Pakistan	1988-90 1993-96	1947	10.5	developing	PM	0.0
Brundtland, Gro Harlem	Norway	1981 1986-89 1990-96	1913	36.0	advanced	PM	47.4
Campbell, Kim	Canada	1993	1918	13.7	advanced	PM	18.0
Chammoro, Violeta	Nicaragua	1990-96	1955	16.0	developing	P	0.0

Charles, Mary Eugenia	Dominica	1966-77 1980-	1951	5.0	developing	PM	9.1
Ciller, Tansu	Turkey	1993-96	1934	1.3	developing	PM	3.6
Cresson, Edith	France	1991-92	1944	7.7	advanced	PM	12.1
Domitien, Elizabeth	Central African Republic	1975-76	na	na	developing	PM	5.6
Finnbogadóttir, Vigdis	Iceland	1980-96	1915	22.1	advanced	P	9.1
Gandhi, Indira	India	1966-77 1980-84	1950	8.8	developing	PM	6.2
Liberia-Peters, Maria	Netherlands Antilles	1984-86 1988-	na	na	developing	PM	na
Meir, Golda	Israel	1969-74	1948	5.8	advanced	PM	0.0
Pascal-Trouillot, Ertha	Haiti	1990	na	na	developing	P	na
Perón, Isabel	Argentina	1974-76	1952	20.0	developing	P	0.0
Pintasilgo, Maria de Lourdes	Portugal	1979	1976	9.2	advanced	PM	0.0
Planinc, Milka	Yugoslavia	1982-86	1946	15.6	advanced	PM	0.0

Comparison of Women National Leaders (continued)

Prunskiene, Kazimiera	Lithuania	1990-91	na	na	advanced	PM	na
Robinson, Mary	Ireland	1990-97	1918	18.0	advanced	P	7.1
Suchocka, Hanna	Poland	1992-93	1918	12.1	advanced	PM	0.0
Thatcher, Margaret	England	1979-90	1918	6.4	advanced	PM	0.0
Zia, Khaleda	Bangladesh	1991	1947	10.0	developing	PM	8.3

Sources: Guida M. Jackson. *Women Who Ruled* (Santa Barbara, CA: ABC-CLIO, 1990); Francine D'Amico and Peter R. D'Amico, eds. *Women in World Politics: An Introduction* (Westport, CT: Bergin & Garvey, 1995); Michael A. Genovese, ed. *Women as National Leaders* (London: Sage Publications, 1993).
Notes: Prime Minister is indicated by PM; President is indicated by P.

Selected Bibliography

ARTICLES, BOOKS, AND REPORTS

Ackelsberg, Martha, and Irene Diamond. "Gender and Political Life: New Directions in Political Science," in Beth B. Hess and Myra M. Ferree, eds. *Analyzing Gender: A Handbook of Social Science Research*. Newbury Park, CA: Sage Publications, 1987, pp. 504-25.

Alexander, Deborah, and Kristi Andersen. "Gender as a Factor in the Attribution of Leadership Traits." *Political Research Quarterly* 46 (September 1993), 527-45.

Aquino, Belinda A. "Democracy in the Philippines." *Current History* 88 (April 1989), 181-202.

Astin, Helen S., and Carole Leland. *Women of Influence, Women of Vision: A Cross-Generational Study of Leaders and Social Change*. San Francisco, CA: Jossey-Bass Publishers, 1991.

Beckman, Peter R., and Francine D'Amico, eds. *Women, Gender, and World Politics: Perspectives, Policies, and Prospects*. Westport, CT: Bergin & Garvey, 1994.

Bem, Sandra L. *The Lenses of Gender: Transforming the Debate on Sexual Inequality*. New Haven, CT: Yale University Press, 1993.

Berentsen, Kirsten K. "Drivkraften bak Gro." *Magasinet SAS Norge*, no. 4 (Summer 1995), 9-15.

Bergman, Solveig. "Nordic Cooperation in Women's Studies." *Womens Studies Quarterly* 20, nos. 3-4 (Fall/Winter 1992), 58-67.

Bhutto, Benazir. *Daughter of the East.* London, England: Hamish Hamilton, 1988.

Bjorklund, Tor. *Holdning til likestilling.* Arbeidersnotat 5/85. Oslo, Norway: Institutt for samfunnsforskning, 1985.

Boneparth, Ellen, and Emily Stoper, eds. *Women, Power and Policy: Toward the Year 2000.* 2nd ed. New York: Pergamon Press, 1988.

Booth, John A., and Thomas W. Walker. *Understanding Central America.* Boulder, CO: Westview Press, 1989.

Bowker-Saur. *Who's Who of Women in World Politics.* New York: Bowker-Saur, 1991.

Brill, Alida, ed. *A Rising Public Voice: Women in Politics Worldwide.* New York: Feminist Press, 1995.

Brundtland, Gro Harlem. "Global Change and Our Common Future." *Environment* 31 (June 1989), 16-43.

Brundtland, Gro Harlem. "Global energipolitkk. Et norsk syn." *Internasjonal Politikk,* nos. 5-6 (1987), 23-34.

Brundtland, Gro Harlem. *Kvinners Europa.* A-Info 30/94. Oslo, Norway: Arbeiderbevegelsen, 1994.

Brundtland, Gro Harlem. *Mitt Liv, 1939-1986.* Oslo, Norway: Gyldendal, 1998.

Brundtland, Gro Harlem. "In Tune with Nature." *World Health* (January-February 1990), 4.

Brustad, Sylvia. *Kjerringråd for kvinneliv.* A-Info 2/95. Oslo, Norway: Arbeiderbevegelsen, 1995.

Burki, Shahid Javed. "Pakistan's Cautious Democratic Course." *Current History* 91 (March 1992), 117-22.

Burns, James MacGregor. *Leadership.* New York: Harper & Row, 1978.

Burrell, Barbara. "The Political Leadership of Women and Public Policy-making." *Policy Studies Journal* 25, no. 4 (Winter 1997), 565-69.

Byrne, Lesley H. "Feminists in Power: Women Cabinet Ministers in the New Democratic Party (NDP) Government of Ontario, 1990-1995." *Policy Studies Journal* 25, no. 4 (Winter 1997), 601-13.

Bystydzienski, Jill M. *Women in Electoral Politics: Lessons from Norway.* Westport, CT: Praeger, 1995.

Bystydzienski, Jill M., ed. *Women Transforming Politics: Worldwide Strategies for Empowerment.* Bloomington: Indiana University Press, 1992.

Cantor, Dorothy W., Toni Bernay, and Jean Stoess. *Women in Power: The Secrets of Leadership.* New York: Houghton Mifflin, 1992.

Chamorro, Violeta Barrios de. "The Death of La Prensa." *Foreign Affairs* 65, no. 2 (Winter 1986/87), 383-86.

Chodrow, Nancy Julia. "Gender, Relation, and Difference," in Hester Eisenstein and Alice Jardine, eds. *The Future of Difference.* New Brunswick, NJ: Rutgers University Press, 1985, pp. 3-19.

Chua-Eaon, Howard G. "All in the Family." *Time* (Fall 1990), 33-34.

Coole, Diana H. *Women in Political Theory: From Ancient Misogyny to Contemporary Feminism.* Boulder, CO: Lynne Rienner Publishers, 1988.

Council of Women World Leaders. Transcript from 1998 Summit of the Council of Women World Leaders, John F. Kennedy School of Government, Harvard University. Located at the following URL address on the Internet: http://www.ksg.harvard.edu/ksgpress/ksg_news/transcripts/cwwl.htm.

Crapol, Edward P., ed. *Women and American Foreign Policy: Lobbyists, Critics, and Insiders.* 2nd ed. Wilmington, DE: Scholarly Resources, 1992.

D'Amico, Francine, and Peter R. D'Amico, eds. *Women in World Politics: An Introduction.* Westport, CT: Bergin & Garvey, 1995.

DeFronzo, James. *Revolutions and Revolutionary Movements.* Boulder, CO: Westview Press, 1991.

Deutchman, Iva Ellen. "The Politics of Empowerment." *Women & Politics* 11, no. 2 (1991), 1-18.

Dougherty, James E., and Robert L. Pfaltzgraff, Jr. *Contending Theories of International Relations.* Philadelphia: Lippincott, 1971.

Eagly, Alice H., Mona G. Makhijani, and Bruce G. Klonsky. "Gender and the Evaluation of Leaders: A Meta-Analysis." *Psychological Bulletin* 111, no. 1 (1992), 3-22.

Edmisten, Patricia Taylor. *Nicaragua Divided: La Prensa and the Chamorro Legacy.* Pensacola: University of West Florida Press, 1990.

Eisenstein, Hester, and Alice Jardine, eds. *The Future of Difference.* New Brunswick, NJ: Rutgers University Press, 1985.

Ferraro, Geraldine A. *Changing History: Women, Power, and Politics.* Wakefield, RI: Moyer Bell, 1993.

Flax, Jane. "Postmodernism and Gender Relations in Feminist Theory." *Journal of Women in Culture and Society* 12, no. 4 (1987), 621-43.

Forbes, Beverly A. "Profile of the Leader of the Future: Origins, Premises, Values and Characteristics of the Theory F Transformational Leadership Model." Mimeograph. Seattle: University of Washington, 1991.

Forcey, Linda Rennie. "Women as Peacemakers." *Peace & Change* 16, no. 4 (October 1991), 331-54.

Fougner, Brit, and Mona Larsen-Asp, eds. *Norden–kvinners paradis?* Copenhagen, Denmark: Nordisk Ministerråd, 1994.

Gardner, Marilyn. "World Leaders' Council: Only Women Need Apply." *Christian Science Monitor*, 8 October 1997, p. 13.

Genovese, Michael A., ed. *Women as National Leaders.* London: Sage Publications, 1993.

Gibbs, Nancy. "Norway's Radical Daughter." *Time* (25 September 1989), 43-44.

Gilligan, Carol. "In a Different Voice: Women's Conceptions of Self and of Morality," in Hester Eisenstein and Alice Jardine, eds. *The Future of Difference.* New Brunswick, NJ: Rutgers University Press, 1985, pp. 274-317.

Gilligan, Carol. *In a Different Voice: Psychological Theory and Women's Development.* Cambridge, MA: Harvard University Press, 1982.

Gray, John. *Men Are from Mars, Women Are from Venus: A Practical Guide for Improving Communication and Getting What You Want in Your Relationships.* New York, NY: HarperCollins, 1992.

Gupte, Pranay. "OPEC's Scandinavian Partner." *Forbes* (15 December 1986), 144-46.

Haavio-Mannila, Elina, Drude Dahlerup, Maud Eduards, Esther Gudmundsdóttir, Beatrice Halsaa, Helga Maria Hernes, Eva Hänninen-Salmelin, Bergthora Sigmundsdóttir, Sirkka Sinkkonen, and Torild Skard, eds. *Unfinished Democracy: Women in Nordic Politics.* New York: Pergamon Press, 1985.

Hansson, Steinar, and Ingolf Håkon Teigene. *Makt og Mannefall: Historien om Gro Harlem Brundtland.* Oslo, Norway: J.W. Cappelens Forlag, 1992.

Hare-Mustin, Rachel T., and Jeanne Marecek, eds., *Making a Difference: Psychology and the Construction of Gender*. New Haven, CT: Yale University Press, 1990.

Harris, Ian M. *Peace Education*. Jefferson, NC: McFarland, 1988.

Harstock, Nancy C. M. "Prologue to a Feminist Critique of War and Politics," in Judith Hicks Stiehm, ed. *Women's Views of the Political World of Men*. Dobbs Ferry, NY: Transnational Publishers, 1984, pp. 123-50.

Haskel, Barbara, G. *The Scandinavian option: Opportunities and Opportunity Costs in Postwar Scandinavian Foreign Policies*. Oslo, Norway: Universitetsforlaget, 1976.

Hauptfuhrer, Fred. "On Top of the World." *People* (20 April 1987), 35-39.

Held, Virginia. *Feminist Morality: Transforming Culture, Society, and Politics*. Chicago: University of Chicago Press, 1993.

Hernes, Helga M. *Welfare State and Woman Power: Essays in State Feminism*. Olso, Norway: Norwegian University Press, 1987.

Hess, Beth B., and Myra M. Ferree, eds. *Analyzing Gender: A Handbook of Social Science Research*. Newbury Park, CA: Sage Publications, 1987.

Higonnet, Margaret R., Jane Jenson, Sonya Michel, Margaret C. Weitz, eds. *Behind the Lines: Gender and the Two World Wars*. New Haven, CT: Yale University Press, 1987.

Hirsti, Reidar, ed. *Gro: Midt i Livet*. Oslo, Norway: Tiden Norsk Forlag, 1989.

Hoel, Sigrun. "Moving Towards Real Rights for Women—The Legal Strategy." Mimeograph. Oslo, Norway: Norwegian Labor Party, 1994.

Huddy, Leonie, and Nayda Terkildsen. "The Consequences of Gender Stereotypes for Women Candidates at Different Levels and Types of Office." *Political Research Quarterly* 46 (September 1993), 503-25.

Hurwood, Bernhardt J. "Iceland's Optimist." *Christian Science Monitor*, 16 September 1982, p. 15.

Inglehart, Ronald, and Pippa Norris. "Gender Gaps in Voting Behavior in Global Perspective." 3 September 1997 paper residing on the John F. Kennedy School of Government, Harvard University, world wide website: http://www.ksg.harvard.edu/ people/pnorris /APSA98_31_6.htm.

Jackson, Guida M. *Women Who Ruled.* Santa Barbara, CA: ABC-CLIO, 1990.

Jagland, Thorbjørn. *Verdier og likestilling.* A-Info 3/95. Oslo, Norway: Arbeiderbevegelsen, 1995.

Janeway, Elizabeth. "Women and the Uses of Power," in Hester Eisenstein and Alice Jardine, eds. *The Future of Difference.* New Brunswick, NJ: Rutgers University Press, 1985, pp. 327-44.

Jaquette, Jane S., ed. *Women in Politics.* New York: Wiley, 1974.

Johnson, Paula. "Women and Power: Toward a Theory of Effectiveness." *Journal of Social Issues* 32, no. 3 (1976), 99-110.

Kahn, Kim Fridkin. "Gender Differences in Campaign Messages: The Political Advertisements of Men and Women Candidates for U.S. Senate." *Political Research Quarterly* 46 (September 1993), 481-502.

Karvonen, Lauri, and Per Selle, eds. *Women in Nordic Politics: Closing the Gap.* Brookfield, VT: Dartmouth Publishing, 1995.

Kelber, Mim, ed. *Women and Government: New Ways to Political Power.* Westport, CT: Praeger, 1994.

Kerber, Linda K. "Separate Spheres, Female Worlds, Woman's Place: The Rhetoric of Women's History." *Journal of American History* 75 (June 1988), 4-39.

King, Martin Luther, Jr. *Where Do We Go from Here? Chaos or Community.* New York: Harper and Row, 1967.

Klenke, Karin. *Women and Leadership: A Contextual Perspective.* New York: Springer Publishing, 1996.

Kriesberg, Louis. "Conflict Resolution Applications to Peace Studies." *Peace & Change* 16, no. 4 (October 1991), 400-417.

Leahy, Margaret E. *Development Strategies and the Status of Women.* Boulder, CO: Lynne Rienner, 1986.

Lee, Shin-wha, ed. *International Directory of Women's Political Leadership, 1991-92.* College Park, MD: Center for Political Leadership and Participation, 1992.

Lerner, Gerda. "New Approaches to the Study of Women in American History." *Journal of Social History* 3, no. 1 (Fall 1969), 53-62.

Lipman-Blumen, Jean. *Gender Roles and Power.* Englewood Cliffs, NJ: Prentice-Hall, 1984.

Lips, Hilary M. *Women, Men, & the Psychology of Power.* Englewood Cliffs, NJ: Prentice-Hall, 1981.

Manor, James. "Innovative Leadership in Modern India: M. K. Gandhi, Nehru, and I. Gandhi," in Gabriel Sheffer, ed. *Innovative Leaders in International Politics*. Albany: State University Press of New York, 1993, pp. 187-215.

Marquand, Robert. "Women at Pinnacle of Power." *Christian Science Monitor*, 1 May 1998, p. 1.

Matland, Richard E. "The World's Leader in Female Representation: Norway," in Shin-wha Lee, ed. *International Directory of Women's Political Leadership, 1991-92*. College Park, MD: Center for Political Leadership and Participation, 1992, pp. 163-67.

McCoy, Jennifer L. "Nicaragua in Transition." *Current History* 90 (March 1991), 117-32.

Millet, Richard L. "Nicaragua: A Glimmer of Hope?" *Current History* 89 (January 1990), 21-37.

Montagu, Ashley. *The Natural Superiority of Women*. New York: Macmillan, 1992.

Morgen, Sandra, and Ann Bookman. "Rethinking Women and Politics: An Introductory Essay," in Sandra Morgen, and Ann Bookman, eds. *Women and the Politics of Empowerment*. Philadephia, PA: Temple University Press, 1988, pp. 3-29.

Morgen, Sandra, and Ann Bookman, eds. *Women and the Politics of Empowerment*. Philadephia, PA: Temple University Press, 1988.

Moyers, Bill. *A World of Ideas with Bill Moyers*. "Changing Agendas with Gro Harlem Brundtland." Public Affairs Television, New York, 1990. (30 minutes).

Nelson, Barbara J., and Najma Chowdhury, eds. *Women and Politics Worldwide*. New Haven, CT: Yale University Press, 1994.

Norris, Pippa. "Choosing Electoral Systems: Proportional, Majoritiarian and Mixed Systems." *International Political Science Review* 18, no. 3 (July 1997), 297-312.

Nyhamar, Jostein. *Arbeiderbevegelsens Historie i Norge*. Oslo, Norway: Arbeiderbevegelsen, 1990.

Okin, Suan Moller. *Women in Western Political Thought*. Princeton, NJ: Princeton University Press, 1979.

Opfell, Olga S. *Women Prime Ministers and Presidents*. Jefferson, NC: McFarland, 1993.

Papandreou, Margarita. "Feminism and Political Power: Some Thoughts on a Strategy for the Future," in Ellen Boneparth and Emily Stoper, eds. *Women, Power and Policy: Toward the Year 2000*. 2nd ed. New York: Pergamon Press, 1988, pp. xi-xix.

Pateman, Carole. "'Does Sex Matter to Democracy?'—A Comment." *Scandinavian Political Studies* 13, no. 1 (1990), 57-63.

Pond, Elizabeth. "Women in Leadership: A Letter from Stockholm." *The Washington Quarterly* 19, no. 4 (Autumn 1996), 59-69.

Randall, Vicky. *Women and Politics: An International Perspective*. 2nd ed. Chicago: University of Chicago Press, 1987.

Richter, William L. "Pakistan under Benazir Bhutto." *Current History* 88 (December 1989), 433-51.

Rosenbach, William E., and Robert L. Taylor, eds. *Contemporary Issues in Leadership*. 2nd ed. Boulder, CO: Westview Press, 1989.

Rosenberg, Emily. "Gender." *Journal of American History* 77, no. 1 (June 1990), 116-24.

Rule, Wilma. "Women's Underrepresentation and Electoral Systems," *Political Science & Politics* 27, no. 4 (December 1994), 689-93.

Safir, Marilyn, Martha T. Mednick, Dafne Israell, and Jessie Bernard, eds. *Women's Worlds: From the New Scholarship*. New York: Praeger, 1985.

Saint-Germaine, Michelle A. "Women in Power in Nicaragua: Myth and Reality," in Michael A. Genovese, ed. *Women as National Leaders*. London: Sage Publications, 1993, pp. 70-102.

Sardar, Ziauddin. "Kept in Power by Male Fantasy." *New Statesman* 127, no. 4397 (Summer 1996), 24-26.

Schein, Virginia E. "Would Women Lead Differently?" in William E. Rosenbach and Robert L. Taylor, eds. *Contemporary Issues in Leadership*. 2nd ed. Boulder, CO: Westview Press, 1989, pp. 154-60.

Schuster, Ilsa. "Political Women: The Zambian Experience" in Marilyn Safir, Martha T. Mednick, Dafne Israell, and Jessie Bernard, eds. *Women's Worlds: From the New Scholarship*. New York: Praeger, 1985, pp. 189-98.

Scott, Joan. "Deconstructing Equality-Versus-Difference: Or, the Uses of Post-structuralist Theory for Feminism." *Feminist Studies* 14, no. 1 (Spring 1988), 33-50.

Sheffer, Gabriel, ed. *Innovative Leaders in International Politics*. Albany: State University of New York Press, 1993.

Skjeie, Hege. "On Authority: Weberian Ideal Types and Norwegian Politics," in *Politics: A Power Base for Women?* Örebro Women's Studies, no. 3. Report from a conference in Örebro, Sweden, 12-16 May 1993.

Skjeie, Hege. "Politisk Lederskap." *Nytt Norsk Tidsskrift* 2 (1992), 118-35.

Skjeie, Hege. "The Feminization of Power: Norway's Political Experiment (1986-)." Oslo, Norway: Institut for Samfunsforskning Rapport, August 1988.

Skjeie, Hege. "The Rhetoric of Difference: On Women's Inclusion into Political Elites." *Politics and Society* 19, no. 2 (June 1991), 233-63.

Skjeie, Hege. "The Uneven Advance of Norwegian Women." *New Left Review* 187 (May/June 1991), 79-102.

Solheim, Bruce O. *The Nordic Nexus: A Lesson in Peaceful Security.* Westport, CT: Praeger, 1994.

Steinem, Gloria. "Gro Harlem Brundtland." *Ms* (January 1988), 74-75.

Stiehm, Judith Hicks, ed. *Women's Views of the Political World of Men.* Dobbs Ferry, NY: Transnational Publishers, 1984.

Stimpson, Catharine. *Where the Meanings Are.* New York: Routledge, 1990.

Takala, Annika. "Feminist Perspectives on Peace Education." *Journal of Peace Research* 28, no. 2 (1991), 231-35.

Thomas, Sue. *How Women Legislate.* New York: Oxford University Press, 1994.

Thomas, Sue, and Clyde Wilcox, eds. *Women and Elective Office: Past, Present, and Future.* New York: Oxford University Press, 1998.

Tovsen, Marit. "Women in Politics in Norway. Seminar paper for Women from Eastern Europe, Denmark, 19 August 1992, mimeograph.

Tronto, Joan C. "Beyond Gender Difference to a Theory of Care." *Journal of Women in Culture and Society* 12, no. 4 (1987), 644-63.

Turner, Lynn H., and Helen M. Sterk, eds. *Differences That Make a Difference: Examining the Assumptions in Gender Research.* Westport, CT: Bergin & Garvey, 1994.

Weigert, Kathleen Maas. "Peace Studies as Education for Nonviolent Social Change." *Annals of the American Academy of Political and Social Science* 504 (July 1989), 37-47.

Weiner, Eric. "Where Women Rule, They Leave Genderless Legacy Behind." *Christian Science Monitor*, 10 May 1995, p. 1.

Zakaria, Rafiq. *Women & Politics in Islam: The Trial of Benazir Bhutto.* New York: New Horizons Press, 1989.

GOVERNMENT DOCUMENTS

Brundtland, Gro Harlem. Curriculum Vitae. Prime Minster's Office, Oslo, Norway, 1994, mimeograph.
Nordic Council of Ministers. *Women and Men in the Nordic Countries: Facts and Figures 1994.* Copenhagen, Denmark: Nord 1994:3.
Norwegian Equal Status Ombud. "The Norwegian Equal Status Act With Comments." 1989, Oslo, Norway.
Norwegian Equal Status Council. "Women in Politics: Equality and Empowerment." 1994, Oslo, Norway.
Norwegian Labor Party. "Protokoll fra Landskvinnekonferansen 1989-1990." 1990, Oslo, Norway.
Norwegian Labor Party Women's Movement. "Kvinner og makt." Ny hverdag. Kvinnepolitisk handlingsprogram, March 1985.
Norwegian Labor Party. Beretning, 1987-1992.
Norwegian Royal Ministry of Children and Family Affairs. St. meld. nr. 70 (1991-92). Likestillingspolitikk for 1990-åra. Oslo, Norway.
Norwegian Royal Ministry of Children and Family Affairs. "Gender Equality in Norway." The National Report to the Fourth UN Conference on Women in Beijing, October 1994. Oslo, Norway.
Norwegian Royal Ministry of Children and Family Affairs. "Growing Up in Norway." Oslo, Norway.

NEWSPAPERS AND MAGAZINES

Aftenposten (Oslo, Norway). Daily newspaper.
Arbeiderbladet (Oslo, Norway). Daily newspaper.
Christian Science Monitor
Economist
Folkevett (Oslo, Norway). Monthly magazine.
Forbes
Journalisten (Oslo, Norway). Quarterly journal.
Kapital (Oslo, Norway). Quarterly journal.
Los Angeles Times
Miljø (Oslo, Norway). Quarterly journal.
Mother Jones
Ms.
New York Times
News of Norway (Washington, DC). Monthly newspaper.
Newsweek

People
Seattle Times
Time
Unesco Courier (New York). Monthly magazine.
U.S. News and World Report
Verdens Gang (VG) (Oslo, Norway). Daily newspaper.
Vogue
Wall Street Journal
Washington Post
Western Viking (Seattle, WA). Weekly newspaper.

PERSONAL INTERVIEWS AND PUBLIC ADDRESSES

Berget, Grete. State Cabinet Minister for Family and Children, Oslo, Norway. Interview conducted 30 June 1995.

Cross, Virginia. President of Muckleshoot Tribal Council, Auburn, Washington. Panel discussion on 10 March 1995 at International Women's Leadership Conference, Green River Community College, Auburn, Washington.

Gates, Mary. Mayor of Federal Way, Washington. Panel discussion on 10 March 1995 at International Women's Leadership Conference, Green River Community College, Auburn, Washington.

Skartveit, Hanne. Political Editor, *Verdens Gang (VG)*, Oslo, Norway. Interview conducted 29 June 1995 in Oslo.

Skeije, Hege. Researcher, Institutt for Samfunnsforskning, Oslo, Norway. Interview conducted 28 June 1995 in Oslo.

Solberg, Erna. Member of Parliament, Bergen, Norway. Interviews conducted 8-10 March 1995 in Seattle, Washington.

Solberg, Erna. "Women Leaders and Gender Partnerships in a Transforming Global Society." Address at International Leadership Conference. Green River Community College, Auburn, WA, March 1995.

Strand, Arne. Deputy Chief Editor, *Arbeiderbladet,* Oslo, Norway, and former State Secretary for Prime Minister Gro Harlem Brundtland, 1987-1989. Interview conducted on 3 July 1995 in Oslo.

Width, Henrik. Political Editor, *Aftenposten*, Oslo, Norway. Interview conducted 27 June 1995 in Oslo.

Index

About the Author

BRUCE O. SOLHEIM teaches American History at Citrus College in
Glendora, California.

ISBN 0-313-31000-9

EAN

9 780313 310003

HARDCOVER BAR CODE